My Soul Is a Woman

My Soul
Is a Woman

The Feminine in Islam

Annemarie Schimmel

Translated by
Susan H. Ray

CONTINUUM | NEW YORK

1997
The Continuum Publishing Company
370 Lexington Avenue, New York, NY 10017

Originally published under the title
Meine Seele ist eine Frau: Das Weibliche im Islam
Copyright © 1995 by Kösel Verlag GmbH & Co., Munich

This translation copyright © 1997 by
The Continuum Publishing Company

Printed in the United States of America

Library of Congress Cataloging-in-Publication Data

Schimmel, Annemarie.
  [Meine Seele ist eine Frau.   English]
  My soul is a woman : the feminine in Islam / Annemarie Schimmel ;
translated by Susan H. Ray.
      p.   cm.
  Includes bibliographical references (p.   ) and index.
  ISBN 0-8264-1014-6
  1. Women in Islam.   I. Title.
BP173.4.S36   1997
297'.082—dc21   97-113267
                                                               CIP

Dedicated to the memory of
Samiha Ayverdi
with gratitude

Contents

Contents

◣ Preface ◢ _____

THE NUMBER OF BOOKS dealing with women in Islam is growing by leaps and bounds: sociological studies are under way, medical problems are being examined, and the positive as well as negative aspects of the harem are under investigation. Works about Arabic and Turkish woman rulers are being researched and written, not to mention those relating to sexual problems and the raising of children. In short, the topic of "the woman in Islam" is now in vogue. Feminists particularly are eagerly trying their hand at it, albeit very frequently without sufficient knowledge of the historical facts and, even worse, to a great extent ignorant of Islamic languages and literatures. Wiebke Walther's impressive study *Women in Islam* still provides a solid foundation for further research. Nor should we omit Sachiko Murata's thought-provoking work *The Tao of Islam*, which examines the relations between the sexes in Islam from the standpoint of a scholar widely read in Islamic jurisprudence as well as its mysticism.

My intention with this book is not to suddenly join the stream of feminist criticism but rather to explore a new approach, one that, I hope, will lead to a better understanding of the woman's role in Islamic mysticism. In the early 1950s Professor Friedrich Heiler, a specialist in the history of religion, held regularly scheduled courses and

seminars on the position of women in various religions. I
had the opportunity to work very closely with him, and
thus owe many new insights to his stimulating discussions.
It was partly the influence of Professor Heiler, then, and
partly because of personal reasons that I published a number of research articles on the woman's place in Sufism in
the early 1950s. This topic, initially and very capably presented by Margaret Smith in her standard work on the
great Rabiʿa (*Rabia the Mystic and her Fellow Saints in
Islam* [1928]), was a source of unending fascination for
me—not only because of its literary importance but also
because I had the personal good fortune of becoming
acquainted with saintly and mystical women leaders in the
Islamic world in the course of visiting the graves of such,
often legendary, women in Turkey, India, and Pakistan. To
one of them, the Turkish mystical writer Samiha Ayverdi
(1906–1993), this book is dedicated in gratitude; I am
indebted to her for many invaluable insights.

As soon as I started this project, I realized how very much
has yet to be done. Another interesting and challenging
study, for example, would be to trace the role women have
played in Islamic scholarship. The number of women in traditional disciplines, which is to say, those active in the
transmission of *hadith*, or the traditions of the Prophet, is
enormous (even if the acceptance of such transmission is
still designated as ʿilm ar-rijal, "knowledge of the men").
Wasn't the youngest wife of the Prophet, ʿAʾisha, a source of
numerous transmissions, especially those having to do
with Muhammad's private life? Since many of the Prophet's
female contemporaries used to interrogate him about theological problems during his lifetime, it should come as no
surprise that the ranks of renowned theologians in later
years included women as well as men. In fact, a Persian
work written around 1600 describes the arguments presented by five women trained in theology, and it does so

primarily to clarify questions concerning certain popular customs and ideas the orthodox religion had rejected. In her study *Women in Islamic Biographical Collections*, Ruth Roded showed that the relatively high percentage of women has remained fairly constant in the biographical works dating from the ninth century right up to our own day.

Another important source of knowledge concerning the lot of women is the *adab* books, edifying guides for young girls that describe the proper deportment of women. One such work was written by the Princess of Bhopal, Shahjahan Begam, in the second third of the nineteenth century: *Tahzibu ʾn-niswan wa tarbiyatu ʿl-insan*, "The Polishing of Women and the Education of Humanity." This was followed in our century by the comprehensive work titled *Bihishti Zewar*, "Paradisiacal Ornament," by Ashraf ʿAli Thanawi. This book formed an integral part of a young Indian girl's dowry for many years. It taught them how to behave properly in all of life's myriad situations, always in keeping with the strict moral and theological precepts of the Deobandi school. Included are guidelines as to how to write respectful letters to one's parents, how to avoid the innumerable superstitious customs that had managed to slip their way into Islam, and how to properly pursue knowledge of the true faith. This book, skillfully and informatively compiled by Barbara D. Metcalf (*Perfecting Women*), is an excellent introduction to the ideals to which a good Muslim maiden was supposed to adhere. Even so, it is best studied in conjunction with the popular novels that began to appear in the Islamic world toward the end of the nineteenth century, for they were also meant to edify their women readers. These works frequently propagate even more progressive ideas than the *adab* books. One example from the Indo-Muslim region is the novel by Deputy Nazir Ahmad, *Mirʿatuʾl-ʿarus*, "The Bride's Mirror." The well-educated and industrious heroine distinguishes herself, among other ways, through acts of charity and beneficence, including the distribution of warm blankets to the poor in winter and passing out Qurans whenever the opportunity presented itself. In the Sindhi tradition, the novel *Zinat* by Mirza Qalich Beg (1892) goes even further than this and describes how one woman well trained in the classical disciplines (that is, Arabic, some history, and basic mathematics) knows how to behave properly and appropriately in every conceivable situation.

In order to fully appreciate the problems confronting the Muslim woman, though, one ought to trace her own literary activities as well. It would take very little effort to compile a comprehensive anthology of verses written by women poets, beginning with the ancient Arabic lamentations women used to sing for their dead brothers (and which can still be found in contemporary Arabic poetry, including such works as those of Fadwa Tuqan, "Lamentations for her Brother"). From these the list would proceed to love lyrics ranging from the frivolous quatrains of the Persian poetess Mahsati up to the lyrical songs of Persian and Turkish women. Furthermore, we should not forget the verses ascribed to princesses and other noblewomen. The Mogul princess Zeb un-nisa (d. 1689) is a particularly good example, while others can be found in Fakhri Harawi's *Jawahir al-ʿajaʾib*, written around 1560 in Sind. In short, such an anthology would show how actively involved with poetry Muslim women of all nationalities were and continue to be.

One could say the same about the women calligraphers whose names are preserved in precious manuscript copies of the Quran and other texts. Likewise and equally worthy of mention are the teachers and professors from whom many great [male] scholars received part of their training.

Nor should we forget the Muslim women involved in the political arena. The wives and mothers of the caliphs were very active in politics, even if not completely publicly, and especially in those areas touching on religion. Louis Massignon's study of the period around 900 is a very informative introduction to this topic. Women rulers are most likely to turn up in the frontier regions of the Islamic world. In fact, Ibn Battuta found a Muslim queen on the Maldivian Islands and mentions rather disapprovingly that women in the North African Tuareg enjoyed an unprecedented amount of freedom. In the Turkish tradition women ruled without hindrance, and this is why the Turkish-born ruler of Delhi, Iltutmish, was able to establish his daughter Razia as his successor in 1236. This was only a few years before Shajarat ad-durr, a former slave woman, began her brief reign in Egypt. Later on, women of India's ruling classes played a leading role not only during the Mogul period but also in the kingdoms of the Deccan. Especially noteworthy is Queen Chand Bibi of Ahmadnagar, who was killed by her own officers in 1600 during the defense of her capital city. Princesses in Delhi and Agra as well as in Golconda and Bijapur were active patrons of architecture, calligraphy, and literature. And wasn't the most famous tomb in the world, the Taj Mahal, erected for a Muslim queen, Mumtaz Mahal, the wife of Shah Jahan, who died in 1631 while giving birth to her fourteenth child? Nor should we forget the political engagement of Muslim women in the Indian war of liberation before 1947!

Another worthwhile project would be an attempt to codify the different ways women are represented in miniature paintings, ranging from the more abstract Persian miniatures to the depiction of women in Persian epics and following through to the lifelike portraits of the Mogul school in India. An analysis of their faces and their clothing would be a highly informative and welcome contribution to Islamic studies.

Also informative would be a study of the honorific titles by which ladies were to be addressed. The handbooks of the secretariat contain explicit regulations as to which lady is to be honored by which form of address, precisely how a letter to her is to be addressed, and similarly important aspects of protocol. Precise norms dating back to the period of the Mamluks in Egypt (1250–1517) are well known and can be found wherever the royal chancellories conducted their business. Fortunately, there are a number of works in Arabic, Persian, Turkish, and Urdu that offer more or less detailed biographies of famous women.

Even while enumerating all these positive aspects, however, we cannot ignore the fact that the woman's position has deteriorated over the course of time. Once flexible regulations have become inflexible and rigid, and negative ideas have gained ground. The Quranic assertion (Sura 2:228) that "men are above women" has been interpreted in an increasingly degrading direction over the years, with the result that many of a woman's vested rights have been curtailed. Women who never learned how to read and write were frequently left in the dark by calculating jurists as far as their rights of inheritance, the possibilities of a divorce, and such matters were concerned. The longer the thought persisted that women were not supposed to know how to read or write, the more it took hold, despite the knowledge that at least one of the Prophet's wives did possess such skills. And yet the question continues to be debated right up to our times in the form of *fatwas*, or "legal opinions or decisions."

Popular folk literature is replete with stories about the cunning of women. This fact alone, however, is hardly reason enough to substantiate an imputed, specifically Muslim attitude toward women based on such tales, for they are not unknown in the Western tradition either. More deserving of serious attention are the theologians' attempts to determine whether women are blessed in paradise with the *visio beatifica*, the beatific sight of God (a question, by the way, that has always posed problems for theologians). Indeed, can they even enter paradise at all, given that, according to one of the sayings attributed to the Prophet, women make up the majority of the inhabitants of hell? Another remark ascribed to the Prophet contradicts this negative view: one day a little old woman anxiously asked him whether such miserable creatures as she might enter paradise. Muhammad said "no," but added with a smile: "for they will all be transformed into beautiful virgins."

Equally important is the fact that the ideal in Muslim society is the *married* woman, and, more important yet, the mother. One of the Prophet's most frequently cited sayings puts it this way: "If it were allowed that anyone prostrate himself before another human being, I would say that wives should prostrate themselves before their husbands."[1] This certainly does not sound like equal rights, but doesn't the Bible also say: "He shall be your Lord!"?

All of this notwithstanding, there is one area in which the woman does enjoy full equal rights, and that is in the realm of mysticism, even if the perfect woman is still referred to as a "man of God." The admiration for pious and learned, God-fearing women is a familiar component throughout the entire history of Islam, and it is to them that this study now turns its attention, be it to women in the form of actual historical figures or as symbols of the human soul yearning for God.

For the suggestions, support, and encouragement that led to the ideas informing this book I am most grateful to my colleague and successor at Harvard, Professor Ali S. Asani, whose studies on the woman-soul in the devotional literature of the Ismailis opened a totally new field of research. With him as well as with Professor Sachiko

---

[1] Quoted from Annemarie Schimmel, *And Muhammad is His Messenger: The Veneration of the Prophet in Islamic Piety* (Chapel Hill, N.C., 1985), p. 279 n. 39.

Murata, State University of New York at Stony Brook, I have frequently discussed the problem of polarity and the importance of the feminine element in Islam. Dr. Dorothea Duda was indefatigable in her efforts to acquire the rights to the illustrations included in this work. Finally, my gratitude also goes to the theologian Anton Kenntemich for interesting references. He passed away before seeing the translation.

Annemarie Schimmel
All Souls Day 1994

⏤ Introduction ⏤

And my soul is a woman before you;
She is like Ruth, Naomi's daughter-in-law.

T HESE ARE THE WORDS Rilke uses to sing of the soul in his
Book of Hours. The image is a very familiar one to the
Western Christian reader: the loving young woman or virgin
(like Ruth) who offers her love in humility, or who (like Sula-
mith in the Song of Solomon) cries after her beloved with
passion and intensity, or those countless women who
thought of themselves as the "handmaidens of the Lord" and
gracefully and unquestioningly accepted his every decree.
The Christian world knows a number of women mystics and
boasts of its ardent singers of God's "*minne*" (= love), among
them the North German Mechthild of Magdeburg. It also
knows women who sought to realize the mystery of the birth
and the care of the Christ Child in their own lives, like Mar-
garete Ebner, as well as women who served God in absolute
devotion and, by doing so, like Teresa of Avila drew others
under the spell of the burning ardor of their heart. There
were also others like Catherine of Siena or Birgitta of
Sweden, who used their God-given powers to intervene in
political events. In short, the theme of the God-loving soul
(the "bride soul" as Peter Hille called it in his nineteenth-
century secular poem of the same name) is a very familiar

one in the West, and the interpretation of the Song of Solomon, especially that of Bernard of Clairvaux, lends such thoughts particular weight.

But how would a Muslim react to Rilke's verse portraying the soul as a humble and loving woman?

Actually, to the consternation of all who see in Islam a purely male-oriented religion, our hypothetical Muslim would have no trouble appreciating Rilke's image at all. Moreover, if he were even slightly acquainted with the literatures of the Islamic languages, these words would immediately call up a flood of associations. For one thing, Islam knows that life cannot exist without the polarity of man and woman (of *yang* and *yin*, as Sachiko Murata calls it in her book *The Tao of Islam*). Second, when the Quran (Sura 2:187) says to the man: "Women are a raiment for you and ye are raiment for them," the phenomenology of religion interprets this to mean that the one is always technically the *alter ego* of the other, simply because a garment (being a portion or an aspect of a person) is frequently used *pars pro toto* to represent the whole person. Furthermore, Sufism, the mystical branch of Islam, is permeated throughout with feminine traits. There is no question but that the imagery employed primarily by the Arabian Sufis is patterned after the classical model of love for an unattainable woman, and there are innumerable Persian verses that tell of the enchantment engendered by a fourteen-year-old boy of otherworldly beauty, a *saqi*, "cup bearer" (frequently referred to as a Christian youth or as a young Zoroastrian). This is a platonic love, of course, but just how powerful it is in determining the image of Sufism, at least in the Persian world, is clearly demonstrated in Hellmut Ritter's comprehensive work called *Das Meer der Seele* (The Ocean of the Soul). The love the mighty king Mahmud of Ghazna (who ruled from 999 to 1030) felt for Ayaz, his military slave, shows how love can turn even a king into the "slave of his slave." This is a theme that crops up in any number of variations in all literary genres.

The biographies of the Sufis list hundreds of "men of God"; in the Arabic world all one need do is think of the hagiographic works of Sulami and Abu Nuʿaim, all of which were composed shortly after the year 1000 and went on to serve as models for later Persian writers. ʿAttar's *Tadhkirat al-auliya* ought to be mentioned in this context as well. It dates from the late twelfth century and was followed three hundred years later by Jami's (d. 1492) *Nafahat al-uns* (actually an expanded version of the first Persian *Lives of the Saints* by ʿAbdullah-i Ansari, d. 1089). These works served as models for later biographies of saints, many of which frequently deteriorated into mere legend, and one can add many subsequent Indian and Turkish works to the list. None of them, however, contain more than a few names of famous women mystics. Unfortunately, Sulami's (d. 1021) book on pious women has been lost.

The two outstanding figures in the history of Sufism were the Andalusian Ibn ʿArabi (1165–1240) and Maulana Jalaluddin Rumi (1207–1273), who hailed from the Turkish-Persian region lying to the north of today's Afghanistan but who spent the greater part of his life in Anatolian Konya. Both had a very particular attitude toward the female element and sometimes showed it in contradictory images.

All classical works and all Sufis, however, eagerly admit that the central figure in the early history of Sufism was a woman by the name of Rabiʿa al-ʿAdawiyya. Tradition has it that it was she who first introduced the element of absolute love of God into the strictly ascetic Sufism of the eighth century. She deserves her place of honor in the history of Islamic mystical love. It was Rabiʿa about whom people said: "When a woman walks in the way of God, she cannot be called a 'woman.'" Such a woman, tradition never tires of reminding us, is a "man," and the use of the word "man" (*rajul* in Arabic, *mard* in Persian, *er* in Turkish) represents an additional difficulty in understanding the role of women in the theory and practice of mysticism. The noun "man" can be used to designate any individual who earnestly strives toward God, without making any direct reference to the biological gender of the individual in question. When the eighteenth-century Sindhi poet Shah ʿAbdul Latif sings of his heroine courageously setting out on the path to her Beloved without paying any attention to the difficulties and sufferings that accompany such a journey, he calls her "manly."

The equating and subsequent identification of the woman with the soul (woman-soul) plays an important role in the literature of the movement. *Nafs*, "soul" or "self," is a feminine noun that appears three times in the Quran in three specific senses: once as the "soul inciting to evil" (Sura 12:53), once as the "accusing soul" (Sura 75:2), and once as the "soul at peace" (Sura 89:27–28). However, the *nafs* is usually compared to a woman who, as the ascetics thought, "incites to evil." To a certain extent, then, the feminine *nafs* in this role can be seen as a mirror image of the secular "world" (*dunya*, likewise a feminine noun), and Muslim writers have made remarks and observations about "Mistress World," who seduces and swallows up men and children, in terms almost as uncomplimentary as those of Christian theologians in the Middle Ages. With them, too, "Mistress World" seeks to divert the man from his intellectual or religious striving, which is just another expression of the typical ascetic male fear of the power of the female.

Nevertheless, the three-tiered nature of the *nafs* hinted at in the Quran provided the basis on which to promulgate a higher estimation of the woman's potential for development. Even a poet like Sanaʾi (d. 1131), who was not exactly favorably disposed toward women, came to say: "A good woman is better than a thousand men." His obvious aversion to the female sex as a whole also led him to comment on the name of the constellation of Ursa Major (the Arabic name of which is *banat an-naʿsh*, "Daughter of the Bier"). According to Sanaʾi, daughters are better dead than alive.

It would be astonishing indeed if Islam were a religion outspokenly inimical toward women, for it was the Prophet Muhammad himself who said in one of his most quoted statements: "God has made dear to me from your world women and fragrance, and the joy of my eyes is in prayer."[1] Women smell nice: "good" (*tayyib*) and "fragrance" (*tib*) both come from the same Arabic root. We should also remember that the Prophet's first wife, Khadija (d. 619), with whom he lived in monogamous union for twenty-five years, supported and comforted him throughout the unprecedented spiritual shock brought about by the initial revelations. Her youngest daughter, Fatima, mother of the Prophet's two grandsons, Hasan and Husain, both martyred for the faith, is the highest and noblest model of womankind in Shiite piety.

The mother motif is of central significance in Islam. Attention has been drawn to the fact that the word *rahma*, "mercy," stems from the same Arabic root as *rahim*, "womb"; it would be completely acceptable, therefore, to speak of the Creator's "maternal love" in its widest sense. "Paradise lies beneath the feet of the mothers" the Prophet said, and one's mother deserves the never-ending care and support of her offspring.

In a similar way, then, the soul can also be represented as a maternal element, and in mystical-theosophic movements every productive act can be looked upon as a "marriage." When iron and flint unite, for example, out of the "union" of these two components arises something higher, namely, fire. It is only when the masculine and the feminine elements collaborate and work together that life can

---

[1] See Annemarie Schimmel, *And Muhammad is His Messenger: The Veneration of the Prophet in Islamic Piety* (Chapel Hill, N.C., 1985), p. 51.

ascend to a higher stage, rather the same way the hard masculine element "fear" and the soft feminine element "hope" "lead to the birth of true faith," as Sahl at-Tustari (d. 896) put it long ago. Intellect, a *yang* element, and the receptive soul, a *yin* element, are inseparably linked, like analysis and synthesis or like "science and love" (to allude to the title of Iqbal's famous Persian poem).

But is there really something in Islamic mysticism that can be directly equated with Rilke's verse cited at the beginning of this chapter? Do women appear as models of the longing soul that expresses its loving devotion in a language all its own? The answer is yes, in fact, for they do appear in this role, and a close study of the data inherent in the mystical literature shows the very interesting development this theme has undergone.

The Quran seldom speaks of women. It was the popular legends that grew up around the Prophet that first portrayed Eve as a temptress, for the Quran itself doesn't even mention her role in the fall from grace. Islam has no conception of original sin as being passed on by biological gender. Nameless women figures are certainly present in the Quran, but only one is identified by her actual name— Mary, or Mariam, the virgin mother of Jesus, who was the last prophet before Muhammad. A favorite among Muslims and especially among mystics the world over, the Virgin Mother is here, as in Christianity, the true handmaiden of the Lord. Sura 19:25 tells how, in the throes of labor, she caught hold of a dried-up palm tree, which immediately showered her with sweet dates. Most important for the later literary development of the theme, however, was a woman known to us from the Old Testament, Zulaikha (Sulaika) by name, the wife of Potiphar, who concentrated all her efforts on seducing Joseph (Yusuf). Countless poets have turned to her as a *nafs* symbol, and it goes without saying that this *nafs* is purified by boundless love and its resultant fathomless sorrow and is finally united with Yusuf. At the end of the road, the indefatigably seeking, unspeakably suffering, loving woman finds the incomparable beauty she so ardently sought manifested in Yusuf. Seen in this light, the story of Yusuf and Zulaikha is the story of the soul yearning passionately for the source of all beauty, for God. And many a seeker (both male and female) has identified with Zulaikha (see below, pp. 44ff).

In classical mystical poetry the Queen of Saba (Sheba) mentioned in Sura 27, whom popular tradition called Bilqis, retreats into the background, and Mary takes on a function of her own, namely, that of a lovely bud that unfolds into the fragrant blossom called "Jesus." But in the work of Islam's greatest mystical poet, Maulana Rumi, all three women appear as symbols of the loving soul. Somewhat earlier even than Rumi, though, was the greatest theosophist (in the classical sense) of the Islamic middle ages, Ibn ʿArabi, who wrote in his mighty *Futuhat al-makkiyya* that women could attain the highest mystical rank. He drew attention to the fact that not only a negatively loaded word like *nafs* was of feminine gender, but so was the word *dhat*, "essence, nature." This only goes to show that in God is contained the creative masculine as well as the receptive feminine element, and without the feminine mirror, which is how he defined the created universe, God would not be able to contemplate His own beauty. Ibn ʿArabi placed such strong emphasis on the central role of the feminine in the world that modern Muslim critics have accused him of tending toward "parasexual symbolism." Nevertheless, his belief that the feminine element was inextricably linked to the masculine (wasn't Eve a part of Adam?) continued to exercise its influence for a very long time.

The image of the "bridal soul" is most clearly defined in the mystical tradition of the Indo-Pakistani region. But it would be simplistic to see in this no more than an automatic takeover of the idea of the *virahini* so central to the

Indian tradition, and especially to *bhakti* mysticism. The Indian tradition has it that only women can really experience *prema*, "unfulfilled love," and *viraha*, "yearning," and when her beloved, her fiancé, or her husband is far away, she suffers unutterable pains of separation. The Indian poetical form of the *barahmasa*, the "Twelve Month Poem," expresses the feelings of the yearning woman during the course of the year. The same motifs can also be found in the sagas and legends of the Indus Valley and the Punjab. In Sindhi and Panjabi literature, the hero is always a woman; she is the one who seeks the beloved and is finally united with him in death after enduring endless trials and tribulations. She remains true to him, the primordial friend, even under the most difficult circumstances. Such courageous women could easily be transformed into symbols for the soul. Whether it be Sassi, the young woman who regrets her heedlessness and wanders through the red-hot deserts until she is ultimately transformed into pure love at the end of her journey, or Marui, the young girl who was kidnapped by a mighty potentate but spent all her time in his richly decorated palace thinking about and yearning for her homeland the way the reed pipe yearns for the reedbank from which it had once been cut—regardless of the individual, what is personified through these woman-souls of the Indo-Pakistani sagas is human experience and mystical theories. The same idea can also be found in the religious literature of the Ismailis, the *ginans*. In the course of time there were also later developments, where the longed-for beloved is, sometimes, the Prophet or the Imam. Love poems, even bridal songs, can be dedicated to the beloved Prophet Muhammad or, as in Ismaili literature, they can even be addressed to the *hazir imam*, the current spiritual leader of the community.

In all of these works the basic pattern remains the same: the soul, represented as and personified by a woman, wanders along the narrow, difficult path that leads to the beloved. The poets sometimes even go so far as to assume a feminine identity for themselves. They call to their (female) "companions"; they watch their "girlfriends" spinning in the courtyard. In fact, even pious dervishes sometimes dressed up as women in order to acquire the additional outward appearance of being "God's handmaiden."

"My Saints are beneath my domes" is an extra-Quranic statement attributed to God and very familiar to Islamic mystics. Bayezid Bistami (d. 874) is credited with the familiar adaptation of this statement referring to the isolation of women whom only very close relatives were allowed to approach: "The saints are the brides of God."

1 · Women and the Prophet

*God has made dear to me from your world
women and fragrance,
and the joy of my eyes is in prayer.*

THIS SAYING OF THE PROPHET MUHAMMAD has been quoted a number of times now—so how is it possible that Islam should have come to be known as a religion with a negative view of women? And yet, over the centuries and under the influence of growing legalistic and ascetic movements, the woman in Islam has been relegated to a position far removed from the one she knew and enjoyed during the times of the Prophet and his successors.

This is why it is impossible to overestimate the role the Prophet's first wife, Khadija, played in defining the woman's place in Islam. This widowed merchant woman was already the mother of several children when she proposed marriage to her significantly younger co-worker Muhammad and subsequently bore his children. She was also the one who consoled and supported him after his first visions and auditions and who convinced him that the revelations he experienced in the cave at Mount Hira during his meditations were not of demonic but rather of divine origin. Khadija rightfully bears the honorary titles Mother of Believers and The Best of Women, *khair un-nisa* (the latter still a favorite name for women). Modern Muslims, including a majority of women Muslims, repeatedly stress her essential contribution to the early history of Islam. She loved Muhammad deeply, and it was only after her death in 619 and after more than a quarter of a century together, that Muhammad gradually and over the course of time married a number of other women. Among his later wives was the very young ʿAʾisha, the daughter of his loyal friend Abu Bakr. The other women were widows or divorcees, some even former slaves. This fact became a very important argument in favor of the remarriage of widows among the modernists in India in the nineteenth and twentieth centuries. Their adherence to Hindu customs had made the Indian Muslims avoid remarriage for a long time, but how could they continue to act in such open contradiction to the Prophet's own example?

The later wives of the Prophet were subsequently given the title Mother of Believers as well. The Quran (Sura 24:30f.) admonished them "to cover their adornments," a regulation probably intended to differentiate them as respectable ladies from the lightly dressed women of the lower classes. Self-concealment dictated by modesty thus became an honor and was not seen as a sign of narrow constraint. It was only over the course of time and as a result of social changes that the rules of seclusion became stricter. In general, they were most rigorously applied to the *sayyid* ladies, which is to say, to those who could trace their descent back to the Prophet and his daughter Fatima. These women were subjected to many other taboos as well, at least in the Indo-Islamic world.

And yet in the early days of Islam women were actively involved in all aspects of social life and communal affairs. ʿAʾisha used to discuss problems arising from tradition with the Prophet's companions, and not only with them. Thus, we have her to thank for our knowledge of many details pertaining to Muhammad's private life. In 656 she actually

rode to battle herself in order to fight against ʿAli ibn Abi
Talib and his partisans. The Sunnite tradition is proud of
ʿAʾisha's activities, and people never tire of citing Muhammad's tender addresses to his young wife—*Kallimini ya
Humaira*, "Talk to me, you little reddish girl" (M I 1972, cf.
M VII, p. 134)—for this young creature was always able to
cheer him up. The mystics, of course, interpreted the
Prophet's kind words as a direct appellation on the part of
the lover to the Divine Spirit, with whom he would like to
speak as if with a—male or female—beloved.

ʿAʾisha is loathed in the Shiite tradition, however, for she
was clearly opposed to ʿAli, the cousin and son-in-law of the
Prophet, the man whom the Shiites honored as their first
Imam, the true Leader of the Community. According to the
Shiites, ʿAli should have been the legitimate successor of
Muhammad after the latter's death, whereas ʿAʾisha's
father Abu Bakr (who ruled from 632-634) had only
usurped the caliphate. Complicating the matter even more
was some bad blood between ʿAʾisha and ʿAli, who had
made some negative remarks about her when she lost her
necklace while on a journey and was brought back to the
caravan by a young man. Doubts about her respectability,
however, were soon dispelled by a revelation (Sura 24:11).
ʿAʾisha's attitude toward ʿAli, whom she confronted in the
already mentioned camel battle that took place in 656,
increased the negative feelings of the Shiites against her.
Her name, so frequently used as a woman's name in Sunnite circles, was never used among the Shiites. In the literature of the ultra-Shiite Nusairis ʿAʾisha is even compared
to the yellowish cow, the sacrifice of which had been offered
to Moses in Sura 2:67–72.

The Prophet had four daughters, and to have daughters
was now no longer considered such a blemish as in pre-
Islamic Arabia, where they used to bury alive what they
considered to be superfluous girls. This immoral practice
was clearly denounced in Sura 81:8. The new appreciation

of daughters was reflected in the fact that men now began adopting a new *kunya*, an agnomen or "honorary name." No longer only calling themselves Abu Talha, "Father of [the boy] Talha" or something along those lines, they now began to call themselves Abu Laila, Abu Raihana, "Father of [the girl] Laila," "Father of [the girl] Raihana," and so on. They did so because, as tradition has it, there is no shame attached to having a daughter. There is even a tradition that congratulates the father, but the reason is likely to surprise the modern reader: after all, a daughter can bring seven sons to the world.

Three of Muhammad's four daughters died during his lifetime: Zainab, Ruqayya, and Umm Kulthum. The latter two were initially married to sons of Abu Lahab, but they left their husbands when Abu Lahab became the Prophet's most bitter adversary (who was even cursed in the Quran [Sura 111]). ʿUthman ibn ʿAffan, who was to become the third caliph (Muhammad's successor from 644 to 656), took them both to wife. Since a simultaneous marriage to sisters is forbidden, he married the one after the early death of the other, and this is why he carries the sobriquet *dhuʾ n-nurain*, "the owner of the two lights." This is also why the combination of names *Osman Nuri* is still popular, especially in Turkey.

The youngest of the Prophet's daughters, Fatima, survived her father by a few months. She was married to Muhammad's cousin, ʿAli ibn Abi Talib, to whom she bore two sons. These boys became the Prophet's beloved grandsons; as tender legends and popular verse tell it, he used to spend many happy hours playing with them. Hasan, the elder of the two, died around 669, probably poisoned, while the younger, Husain, fell in 680 in the Battle of Kerbela against the army of the Umayyad caliph Yazid. The Umayyads had claimed the caliphate for themselves in 661 after the murder of ʿAli, and Husain tried to win power back for the house of the Prophet after Yazid, the second

Umayyad ruler, assumed the position. The tragedy of Kerbela in Iraq, which took place on the tenth day of Muharram (the first lunar month) had a profound effect on Shiite
piety, and if the poetry of the Islamic peoples celebrate the
Prophet's grandsons as glorious heroes, as the first of all
martyrs, then Fatima was also granted a special position
that can be described as nothing less than that of *mater
dolorosa*. Although dead for almost fifty years before the
demise of her second son, Fatima stands higher than all
other people for the Shiites except Muhammad and ʿAli. Her
sobriquets, including *Zahra*, The Radiant One; *Batul*, Virgin; *Kaniz*, Maiden; *Maʿsuma*, Shielded from Sin, and many
others are still very popular names for girls among Shiite
communities. Moreover, not only is she the intercessor for
all who weep for her son Husain, but, in the realm of mystical speculation, she is also the *umm abiha*, "her father's
mother."

Story after story is told about Fatima. Those that dwelt
upon the poverty she endured particularly aroused the fan-
tasy of the pious, for whom she was, in fact, the actual
Queen of Mankind. One literary genre known as "Fatima's
Dowry" (*jihaznama-i Fatima*) enumerates all the humble
trifles her father was able to give her for her dowry, her generosity toward the poor (even when her own family went
hungry), her own sons' want of clothing—and all of this is
related and embellished in ever-new ways, so that Fatima
has come to be a role model for Muslim girls. In fact, in the
Middle Ages there was even a sect that passed the family's
entire fortune on to their daughters as inheritance—and all
in honor of Fatima. Her veneration is also great in the Sunnite world. Whether we read Muhammad Iqbal's (1877–
1938) homage to Fatima in his 1917 Persian epic *Rumuz-i
be-khudi* (Mysteries of Selflessness) (a book, by the way,
that leaves no doubt whatsoever about his Sunni attitudes), or whether we read ʿAli Schariati's "Fatima is

Fatima," which appeared at the time of the Islamic revolution in Iran—all we hear is moving words of praise for this most respected and most virtuous Muslim woman. Only a person descended from her two sons can claim to be a *sayyid*, for this right does not extend to the offspring of ʿAli's other children from other wives.

Most people would probably agree with Sanaʾi (d. 1131 in Ghazna, today's Afghanistan), who sings:

> The world is full of women,
> yet where is there a woman like Fatima,
> the best of women?

for the honorary name The Best of Women, *khair un-nisa*, was later granted not only to Khadija but to her youngest daughter as well.

Among the circles of mystics there were also those who considered the masculine name *Fatir* an appropriate "divine name" for Fatima.

Sources tell of numerous women in the Prophet's close proximity. Several of them emigrated with their families to Abyssinia in the early years of Islam, while others, like Umm ʿAtiya, accompanied Muhammad and his army into a number of battles and cared for the wounded. It was also understood, of course, that they should participate in the prayer service in the mosque, for one *hadith* says: "Do not prevent the handmaidens of God from entering the places in which He is worshiped." Even the second caliph, Omar ibn al-Khattab (ruled 634–644), had to adopt this tradition, albeit not very happily. This ruler was known for his severity and justice and ought to have been more favorably inclined toward women. After all, his sister had already converted to Islam while he was still an apparently irreconcilable opponent of the Prophet. And yet, while intending to kill her during her recitation of Quranic revelations, he was so moved by the words that he immediately accepted Islam

and subsequently became the most zealous defender of the
faith. Even Rumi tells extensively of this conversion in his
prose work *Fihi ma fihi*.

Some of Muhammad's other female descendants are also
known for their piety. One of them, Sayyida Nafisa, is particularly worthy of mention: a great-granddaughter of the
Prophet, she married the son of the sixth imam, Ja'far as-
Sadiq (d. 765), and went to Cairo with her cousin Sakina.
There she soon became known for her ascetic piety. The
historian Ibn Khallikan reports in his biography that even
Imam Shafi'i, the founder of one of the four orthodox
schools of law, is supposed to have said his prayers with
her. Miracles naturally accompanied her wherever she
went. According to one, the water she had used for her ritual ablutions is supposed to have healed a lame Jewess.
When Nafisa died in 208/824, a mausoleum was built in
her memory, and it has remained a popular pilgrim's destination to this day. In the Middle Ages, primarily during the
period of the Mamelukes, the sultans celebrated her birth-
day in great style in the Citadelle of Cairo.

From the very beginning, the Prophet's saying quoted at
the beginning of this chapter as well as his numerous marriages aroused the disapproval of Christian theologians—
and not only theologians! How could a man who claimed to
be the Prophet so abandon himself to the world of sensuality? This idea was simply abhorrent to the Christian ideal of
chastity, to the ideal of celibacy that from early times
onward was so deeply rooted in the church. The Muslim,
however, will see no backsliding in this. Rather, he sees it
as an expression of the joy one can find in the world of the
senses, which is part of God's creation.

An Indo-Muslim interpretation of the Prophet's saying
about "women" and one that derives from the great Delhi
saint Nizamuddin Auliya maintains that the word "women"
refers here very specifically to 'A'isha, whereas "the joy of
my eyes" is said to be a reference to Fatima, who was

absorbed in prayer at the time ("and the joy of my eyes [i.e., Fatima] is at prayer"). This seems a bit farfetched, and we are more easily tempted to credit Ibn ʿArabi's interpretation, according to which the Prophet didn't love women for natural reasons—oh no, "he loved them because God made them lovable." Most important, however, is the reference to fragrance, frequently associated with the feminine element on the one hand and with holiness on the other. As the single masculine concept in Arabic, the word "fragrance" in this saying is inserted between the two feminine nouns "women" and "prayer." This observation was enough to provide the Sufis with never-ending food for thought concerning this mysterious relation.

⟵ 2 · Women in Sufism ⟶

E VEN IF THE WOMAN'S POSITION has deteriorated in many
respects since the days of the Prophet, she continues
to play a very important role in Sufism. This mystical
branch of Islam came into being in the early eighth century,
about a century after the Prophet's death. It was initially a
purely ascetic movement that strove to counteract or work
against the Muslims' increasing worldliness and to remind
them of their religious duties. Sufism gained in strength
and number during the expansionist period of the Islamic
empire. By 711 the Muslims had not only crossed the
Straits of Gibraltar (which still bears the name of its conqueror, *Jabal Tariq,* "the mountain of Tariq"), but had also
penetrated into Sind, the lower Indus Valley (today the
southern part of Pakistan) and had crossed into Trans-
oxiana as well, all on their way to Central Asia.

The ascetics, however, were more interested in conquer-
ing the kingdoms of the heart and the soul, and it is of no
small significance that a central role in this endeavor fell to
a woman. The name of Rabiʿa al-Adawiyya or Rabiʿa of
Basra heralds the beginning of the actual mystical movement in Islam. She is the one credited with having transformed somber asceticism into genuine love mysticism.
Everyone knows the story of how the pious ascetic ran
through Basra with a bucket of water in one hand and a

burning torch in the other, and when asked about the reason behind her actions, she replied: "I want to pour water into hell and set paradise on fire, so that these two veils disappear and nobody shall any longer worship God out of a fear of hell or a hope of heaven, but solely for the sake of His eternal beauty."

This popular legend found its way into the Christian world as well. It was introduced to the West by Joinville, the representative of Louis IX, and was retold by the Quietist Camus in his book *Carité ou la Vraie Charitée*, which appeared in 1640. The illustrations in this work show a woman in oriental dress with a torch and a bucket, over whose head a sun beams with the Hebrew inscription YHWH, thus indicating the Eastern (but not the Islamic!) origin of the story. After that she turns up in every conceivable variation in European literature.

There are innumerable anecdotes surrounding Rabiʿa, the liberated slave girl of Basra. As it happens, Basra was also the home of many other ascetics of the early years. Legends even frequently link the learned and pious preacher Hasan al-Basri (d. 728) to Rabiʿa. The great hagiographers of the Islamic world have devoted long sections of their works to her. In her human perfection she was "clearly superior to many men, and that's why she was also named 'the Crown of Men,'" as Muhammad Zihni writes in his book about famous women (*Meshahir al-Nisa*). To this day a virtuous or otherwise distinguished woman can be described as a "second Rabiʿa."

Rabiʿa has also been credited with countless miracles: her fingertips glowed like lamps at night, and the Kaaba came toward her when she made her pilgrimage (a source of understandable annoyance for another Sufi). She rejected all earthly ties, including marriage, and hovered in the air on her prayer rug. She remained in her chamber one beautiful spring day, and this prompted her maidservant to urge her to go outside and admire God's glorious creation.

Rabi'a is said to have replied that the beauty of God is within, whereas what one can see outside is only a reflection of inner beauty. Rumi attributed this story to an unnamed ascetic and included it in his *Mathnawi* (M IV 1518f.). When 'Attar speaks of the Light of God in his *Ilahi-nama* (XXII), he writes: "And if it shine for a while upon an old woman, it would make her one of the great ones of the world, like Rabi'a."

In the same epic (XV), however, 'Attar tells of her poverty and her suffering:

> For a whole week the saintly Rabi'a had taken no food.
> During that week she never sat down but prayed and fasted
>   continuously.
> When hunger had weakened her legs and utterly exhausted
>   all her limbs and members,
> A woman who lived near her happened to bring her a bowl
>   of food.
> Rabi'a, in pain and suffering as she was, went to fetch a
>   lamp.
> When she returned it chanced that a cat had knocked the
>   bowl upon the ground.
> Again she departed to fetch a pitcher and break her fast
>   with water.
> The pitcher fell from her hand: she was still thirsty and the
>   pitcher was broken.
> That disconsolate one heaved such a sigh that it was as
>   though the whole world had been consumed with fire.
> In utter bewilderment she cried: "O God, what wilt Thou of
>   this poor helpless creature?
> Thou hast cast me into confusion—how long wilt Thou
>   cause me to welter in my blood?"
> There came a Voice saying: "If thou so wish I will this very
>   moment bestow upon thee all that lies between the Moon
>   and the Fish.
> But I shall remove from thy heart the grief that thou hast
>   borne for so many years for My sake. Consider this well.

For not in a hundred years will suffering for Me and this
   deceitful world meet together in a single heart.
If thou wouldst always suffer for Me thou must forsake the
   world forever.
Hast thou the one thou canst not hope for the other, for
   suffering for God is not to be had without paying for it."[1]

It was precisely this, Rabi'a's emphasis on love's affliction
and pain, that the Indian Chishti saint Qutbuddin Bakhtiyar Kaki wrote about in 1235: "When afflicted with pain,
she was happy and said: 'Today my Friend was thinking of
me!,' and should she not perceive such affliction on any
given day, she wept and said: 'What have I done wrong, that
He doesn't think of me?'"

Rabi'a was not the only pious ascetic to devote herself
completely to the love of God. A female relative of the
Prophet, Umm Haram, was already supposed to have par-
ticipated with ardent enthusiasm in the first Muslim expe-
dition against Cypress and is said to have fallen in battle as
a "martyr" in the Holy War (27h/649).

Just about every Sufi handbook contains a more or less
detailed list of the names of early ascetics who passed their
days with weeping and fasting and their nights in prayer.
Margaret Smith introduces us to a number of important figures from the early years in her classic work *Rabia the Mystic and Her Fellow Saints in Islam.*

Among them we find Rabi'a's contemporary, Maryam al-
Basriyya, who died in ecstasy. The contemporary Turkish
poetess Lale Müldür has dedicated a tender poem to her:

> Maryam of Basra
> was Rabi'a's servant girl.
> Hardly had she learned of God's love

[1] Quoted from *The Ilahi-nama or Book of God of Farid al-Din 'Attar,*
translated from the Persian by John Andrew Boyle, with a foreword by
Annemarie Schimmel (Manchester, 1976), p. 153.

than she sank in ecstasy.
During a *dhikr*-meeting
she suddenly died of love.

God has many devotees who, like the rain,
if they fall to earth, turn to corn,
if they fall in the sea, they turn to pearls.

We also know of Bahriyya al-Mausuliyya, who wept herself blind. This is a common motif, for it was felt that physical blindness enables a person to see the Divine Beloved all the better, especially because, as it was later believed, the eye is no longer a veil between the person looking and the one being looked at. Rihana al-Waliha lived in constant ecstasy; others were even confined to madhouses because their love was so all-encompassing that it led to their neglecting the laws of common decency. There were also many other unknown "worshipers of God"—pious, nameless women who turn up again and again in the literature. Many of them sang little songs the way Rabiʿa did. Although not works of art, these were the first examples of a mystical love lyric which, in coming centuries, was to become the characteristic hallmark of the loving Sufi:

A Beloved unlike all others:
He alone has touched my heart.
And although absent from sight and touch,
He is ever present in my heart.

That's the way the Syrian Rabiʿa ash-Shamiya put it. Another example is quoted by Jami:

The lover of God is sick in this world—
his sufferings continue unabated; pain is his only
solace.
Whoever truly loves the Great Creator
wanders through this world with Him on his mind—
and is rewarded with the sight of Him!

The woman who composed this little verse would probably have agreed with Amat al-Jalil, a barely known early Sufi, who said: "The saint knows no instant in which he is occupied with anything other than God. If someone were to attribute another occupation to a saint, he is lying."

Sha'wana is another interesting figure among the early ascetics; she is also famous for her incessant weeping. Even the great ascetic Fudayl ibn 'Iyad (d. 803) is supposed to have asked her to pray for him. The pious Sufi Bishr al-Hafi, known as "The Barefooted One" (d. 841) as well as the great traditionist Ahmad ibn Hanbal (d. 855) approached Amina ar-Ramliyya to ask for her intercession, and it was through her that they learned of their reprieve from hell.

Ghazali tells how Sha'wana appeared to one of her friends in a dream after she (Sha'wana) had died and been highly honored by the inhabitants of paradise. She gave the dreaming woman the following advice: "Let your heart be very sad and let the love of God override your desires. Then nothing will harm you to your dying day."

Thoughts about death and the afterworld are characteristic of the early women ascetics. Another woman who tradition says also came from Basra was Mu'adha. She deprived herself of as much rest as was humanly possible, for the very thought of the long sleep of the grave was enough to keep her awake.

Pious women like these could attain a high rank. It's been said that the Baghdad Sufi Sari as-Saqati (d. ca. 867) brought one of his female followers the news that her son had drowned. She refused to believe him, and shortly thereafter the boy was found alive. The mother's disbelief was based on the fact that she had not received any news of the death of her child from the Invisible One, and "if one listens to God, he learns of everything that concerns him."

This little story shows that Sufi women were by no means all celibate or unmarried, thus following the example set by

Rabiʿa. The outstanding figure among the married Sufi
women is Fatima of Nishapur (d. 849), fifty years younger
than Rabiʿa. She was married to a renowned ascetic,
Ahmad Khidruya (d. 854) and is said to have guided him
often along the mystical path. Legend has it that she was
associated with the great mystical leaders of her time and is
actually supposed to have corresponded with the Egyptian
master Dhuʾn-Nun (d. 859). When he rejected a gift she had
sent him because it came from a woman, she responded
with a sharp reprimand: How could he look at the secondary cause and not at the actual giver, God? Legend also
has it, though, that Dhuʾn-Nun admired her for her com-
prehension of the deeper meaning of the Quran. In fact, in
Dhuʾn-Nun's didactic tales there often appears an
unknown woman or girl filled with the love of God who
teaches him to listen to the praise of God inherent in all of
nature. The wise Fatima is also supposed to have discussed
mystical subjects with Bayezid Bistami (d. 874) and didn't
always bother to wear her veil while doing so. When he
noticed her one beauty spot, a mole, or, according to
another tradition, her henna-stained hands, she discontin-
ued the practice because a purely spiritual association was
now no longer possible. Just how authentic this story is is
hard to say, for the motif of the spiritual friendship
destroyed by a "worldly" glance at the (male or female) com-
panion is no rare theme in hagiography.

Rabiʿa bint Ismail, wife of the Sufi Ahmad ibn Abi al-
Hawari (d. 851), also deserves mention here. As a widow
she wanted to turn the money she had inherited as well as
that which she earned herself to good use, and thus offered
her hand in marriage to the above named Sufi, with whom
she then established a platonic union. She spent her time
in prayer and fasting, all the while caring and providing for
Ahmad and his other wives. For, as she explained to him, "I
do not love you as a spouse, but rather as a brother." And
yet, the wife of Rabah al-Qays is said to have been in the

habit of putting on pretty clothes after saying her evening prayers and of asking her husband if he desired her. If that turned out not to be the case, she returned to her devotions until the dawn's early light.

It was also not uncommon for a pious man to glimpse his future "bride in paradise." Such was the case with ʿAbdul Wahid ibn Zayd (d. 794), who somehow learned where this maiden was to be found. He then spied a shepherdess whose sheep were grazing peacefully under her protection in the midst of a pack of wolves. She was obviously meant for him since—at least this is the way we can interpret the story—her exemplary piety had already realized eschatological peace among the animals on earth. (By the way, I was actually witness to a similar event. A pious Turkish scholar spontaneously declared an older woman, who just happened to be visiting him at the time, to be his wife in paradise. . . .)

The wife of the renowned "theosophist" al-Hakim al-Tirmidhi (d. 936) is particularly interesting. His autobiography reports of his habit of telling her his dreams and visions because she could be relied on to understand their significance. He also relates how an angel told her that both she and her husband had attained the same spiritual rank.

Stories about women minstrels capable of arousing mystical love through their songs are common in classic Arabic literature, and this particular theme continues on in the later Persian transmission. One day the grammarian al-Asmaʿi reprimanded a girl singing about love near the Kaaba. The tables were turned when she taught him about the true love of God. Other examples include the tale of the singing slave girl (the most expensive group of slaves) who earned her freedom because she recited the Quran in such a heartrendingly beautiful way. Another story focuses on a woman minstrel who converted to Islam under the influence of Abu Hafs ʿUmar as-Suhrawardi (d. 1234). It is said that she sang so beautifully before the governor of Hama-

dan upon her return from the pilgrimage that the governor
and all those present repented of their sins and converted
to the true faith, which is to say they readopted a serious
attitude toward Islam. And Rumi's biography tells us that
he was influential in converting "frivolous girls" to mystical
Islam.

It seems that in the early years women were not only
female disciples of great Sufi masters, but they also partic-
ipated in community gatherings devoted to recitations from
the Quran and to *dhikr*, "recollection of God." Fatima, the
daughter of the Sufi al-Kattani (d. 934), is said to have died
in ecstasy during a sermon delivered by the ecstatic Sum-
nun, otherwise known as "the Lover" (d. ca. 900), and three
men died with her. All of this leads to the conclusion that
the woman's participation in such gatherings was nothing
out of the ordinary. Later, of course, there would be long
deliberations as to which legally correct manner was to be
observed in order for a master to initiate a woman into the
order. According to a strict interpretation of the law, the
master was not allowed to touch the skin of an unrelated
woman (or, according to several other schools, he had to
perform a ritual ablution following the ceremony in order to
return to his initial state of ritual purity). This being the
case, they tried dipping the hands of the participants in a
basin of water and having them take the oath this way.
Sometimes the woman was required to grasp the sleeve, a
piece of cloth or even a stick the master held out to her
while taking the oath. In the early years they seemed to
have been a bit more liberal in this regard, as in many
others as well, and we read of mystics who actually even
appeared in public with their female disciples. The eccen-
tric Shibli (d. 945), for example, was said to have taken one
of his female disciples along with him to visit the mystic
Hallaj who was already hanging on a cross at the time.
According to legend, Shibli wanted to ask the master "What
is Sufism?" This story has come down to us via ʿAttar, and

although probably apocryphal, it does show that Sufi women did play a certain public role. Hallaj's own sister appeared after his execution, reprimanded him posthumously for his all-too-daring sayings, and then tossed his ashes into the Tigris as he had requested. That same night, though, her brother appeared to her in a dream and explained his "unorthodox" behavior. (An examination of the role of the sister in the intellectual history of Islam would uncover a great deal of interesting information. In pre-Islamic Arabia, for instance, it was the sister who had to sing the dirge for her brother, and the history of Sufism indicates that important roles and positions continued to be allocated to this immediate female relation. The example of Princess Jahanara, sister of the Heir Apparent of the Mogul Empire, Dara Shikoh, who was executed as a heretic in 1659, is a good example.)

The tradition of pious Sufi women continued in the following centuries, not only in the Middle East, but in the Indian subcontinent as well, where we know of female disciples of Fariduddin Ganj-i Shakar (d. 1265).

In his apologia, ʿAinul Qudat observes that ʿUyaina, the grandmother of the Sufi Abu ʾl-Khair at-Tinani al-Aqtaʿ had five hundred students, both male and female. The biography of the great Hanbalite Sufi ʿAbdullah-i Ansari of Herat (d. 1089) introduces his relative, Bibi Nazanin, who is supposed to have advised him to make the acquaintance of the wise if unlearned Sufi Kharaqani, who was destined to play a decisive role in his own later development.

There were other pious and learned women in Herat at that time renowned mainly for their transmission of the traditions of the Prophet. One such woman, Umm Fadl al-Harmathiya, who died in Herat in 1084, comes particularly to mind. And when Serge de Laugier de Beaureceuil speaks of a "female milieu" interested in the traditions of the Prophet, the Hanbalite school of law and undoubtedly also Sufism along the lines of ʿAbdullah-i Ansari, this corresponds to Louis Massignon's remarks about the Hanbalite women in the circle surrounding the mystic-martyr Hallaj, who continued the traditions about Hallaj for a long time after his death (just as did a certain Zaynab al-Kamaliyya).

Among the extraordinary women traditionists, Karima al-Marwaziyya of Mecca (d. 463/1070) deserves particular attention. She was an ascetic and celibate who, as Massignon says, is connected to the women's *futuwwa* as it is supposed to have been founded by Khadija al-Jahniyya (d. 461/1067). This institution was evidently the female version of the male *futuwwa* sodalities that advocated the ideals of genuine manhood and high-principled life combined with an interiorized worship service. Be that as it may—Karima appears in a whole series of important tradition links revolving around Abu Najib as-Suhrawardi (d. 1165). His nephew, Abu Hafs ꜤUmar as-Suhrawardi, consequently also mentioned her in what has become one of the most widely known standard works of moderate mysticism still studied throughout the Islamic world.

Among the pious and learned women is also one known as Shuhda the Scribe (d. 1176), who was as famous for her transmission as she was for her calligraphy. One hundred and fifty years later the North African traveler Ibn Battuta mentions some women *hadith* teachers in Damascus as well as in Baghdad, namely, Umm Muhammad ꜤAꜣisha and Fatima bint Taj al-Din.

Women who leaned toward the pious, and above all the mystical, life could also be found in Turkey at the time of the Seljuks. Jalaluddin Rumi's relation to the ladies of the upper classes of Konya (such as the wife of the viceroy Aminaddin Mikail) as well as his attractiveness to women of all classes is a fact familiar from his biographies. The wife of the Seljuk monarch Ghiyath al-Din actually carried his likeness around with her. (The proximity of the byzantine artistic tradition can be seen very clearly here in iconoclastic Islam!) And, just as Rumi's second wife Kira Khatun (from a Christian family) was praised by the biographers as "a second Rabi'a, Mary-like," several of his female successors were also engaged in the wider expansion of the Mevlevis, the order organized by his son Sultan Walad (d. 1312), and this included Sultan Walad's own daughter as well. In the Turkish region, the female member of an order was called *baci*, "sister," for "the believers are brothers" (Sura 49:10).

Ibn 'Arabi's attitude toward women is particularly interesting. His memories of the great women ascetics of Seville, whom he had met while still a youth, were very vivid. One, for instance, was Fatima bint al-Muthanna, a woman who lived in extreme poverty. She had been married for many years before her husband died of leprosy. "She was a consolation for the inhabitants of the earth" are the words the Andalusian master used to describe her and to report of her strange miracles. The Sura *al-Fatiha*, the first chapter of the Quran, served her and fulfilled all her desires. So much so, in fact, that she once even restored an unfaithful husband to the wife who had turned to the saint with her pleas for help. Despite her poverty, Fatima, who described herself as Ibn 'Arabi's "spiritual mother" (and whom the biological mother of the great theosophist actually visited on occasion) was possessed of an unflappable cheerfulness. She would sometimes play the tambourine and joyfully praise the glory of God:

> I rejoice in Him, Who has turned toward me and claimed me as one of His Friends, Who has used me for His own purposes. Who am I that He should have chosen me among all of mankind? He is jealous of me, and if I look to others, He loosens afflictions against me.

His admiration for Fatima seems to have prepared Ibn 'Arabi for his particular inclination toward female saints. While in Seville he met yet another remarkable woman, also over eighty. Her name was Shams, the Mother of the Poor,

whom he describes as a high-ranking mystic with extraordinary intuition. She, however, was usually wont to hide
her high spiritual position.

According to Ibn ʿArabi, an unnamed girl slave was
known for her perfect self-discipline: she could cover long
distances in no time flat, carry on conversations with the
mountains and the stones, and used to greet them with
"Welcome!"

These encounters prepared Ibn ʿArabi for his meeting
with an inspiring Persian woman in Mecca. Her name was
Nizam, daughter of the imam of Maqam Ibrahim in the Holy
Place. She met him as he was circumambulating the
Kaaba, lost in ecstasy and reciting verses. The young
woman overheard him and interpreted his verses, to his
great delight. Out of this encounter with the beautiful
woman grew a collection of Ibn ʿArabi's poems known today
as *Tarjuman al-ashwaq* (The Interpreter of Longing). These
poems are written in the traditional style of Arabic love
lyrics that conjures up the standard figures of classical
poetry. The fact that Ibn ʿArabi later felt compelled to eluci-
date these poetic outpourings of his love with a scholarly
mystical-philosophical commentary prepared the way for a
new development in this genre. Not a few later mystics
found it necessary to make their apparently worldly verses
about wine, love, and longing acceptable by appending
their own interpretations to them. In many cases these elu-
cidations destroy the charming balance between the sensuous and the supernatural inherent in the poems and tend to
turn delicate wisplike verses into compendia of metaphysi-
cal scholasticism. In Ibn ʿArabi's case, other poems also
managed to find their way into his later *Diwan*, several of
which may even have been addressed to his earlier wife.
Unfortunately, all of this is shrouded in supposition.

In any case, Nizam seems to have been Ibn ʿArabi's Beat-
rice, for his entire sojourn in the Holy City of Mecca pre-

pared him for his life's work, the *Al-futuhat al-makkiyya*, his "Meccan Revelations."

He met another woman in Mecca as well: Zaynab al Qalᶜiyya. This lady, previously renowned for her beauty and wealth, had retreated into the Holy City, where she was known as an exceptional ascetic who counted many Sufis among her personal friends. Ibn ᶜArabi admired her conscientious performance of devotional duties; in fact, she used to levitate during her meditations. This phenomenon, although not mentioned in the biographies of other women, was probably more widespread than the records would indicate. The fact that she and Ibn ᶜArabi traveled together to Jerusalem shows the high respect he felt for her. His attitude toward women in general is one of the fascinating aspects of the life of this great Andalusian (see pp. 84ff.). Since he felt God had singled him out as the "Seal of the Saints," he also possessed the gift of intercession, and it is interesting to see that the first people for whom he applied this gift while still a young man were all women, namely, his two sisters, his wife at the time, and a fourth woman as well. Unfortunately we know little of this side of his personal life. Fourteen of the fifteen individuals upon whom Ibn ᶜArabi conferred the *khirqa*, or the patched frock of the dervishes (in a purely "spiritual" way, to be sure), were also women. According to Jami's report, he was convinced that women could occupy a place at every stage of the spiritual life. They could even become the *qutb*, the "pole" or "axis," which is the highest rank in the hierarchy of the saints. To the end of his days Ibn ᶜArabi admitted women to his teaching and let them listen while he read from his works.

What kind of life did the women who wanted to enter upon, or even join, the Sufi path lead? On the one hand they could function as benefactresses of a convent and provide shelter and food for a master and his disciples through their financial support. In return, they could be sure of the master's blessing as a token of his gratitude. The patronesses of the convent of Abu Saʿid-i Abuʾl-Khair (d. 1049) in Mihana, Eastern Iran, deserve mention here, especially Bibi Nishi, who produced eye salve. She had her early doubts, but decided to follow the master after overcoming them. In many regions these women were admitted to the communal *dhikr* just as in the early days. In fact, a specific woman's section was constructed for this very purpose in the common rooms of several convents (including that of the Rifaʿiyya in Cairo or those of the Mevlevis in the Ottoman Empire). In other areas women watched the ceremonies from a nearby room or else from the place allotted to them on the roof.

Only one order of dervishes allowed women to participate actively in all rituals, and that was the Bektashi order in Turkey. This understandably gave rise to the accusation of "an immoral way of life" having taken place among the Bektashis. (Incidentally, this same accusation could also be heard when people felt a master was spending too much time alone with a woman while administering the oath or other such rituals.) Yakup Kadri Karaosmanoğlu's novel *Nur Baba* appeared in Istanbul in 1922; it describes the seductive ways of a young Bektashi master and may have contributed to Ataturk's ordering the closure of dervish convents three years later. This theme, however, turns up repeatedly in modern fictional works of social criticism in the Islamic world.

A number of specifically women's convents are known to have existed already in the Middle Ages. They go back to as early as the twelfth century and could be found in Baghdad, Mecca, Medina, Syria, and Cairo. Mecca seems to have been the site of three such institutions (Ribat az-Zahiriyya, Dar Ibn as-Sauda [1194], and Ribat Bint at-Taj). Baghdad, then the center of the Islamic world, was renowned above all else for its Dar al-falak, an institution founded by a woman on the west bank of the Tigris. Other convents followed in 1127 and 1177, and as late as 1254, just four years before the demise of the Abbasid caliphate, the last caliph endowed a convent for women. As it happened, his own daughter was named its first directress. These convents are somewhat reminiscent of the Western charitable institutions established for European gentlewomen.

The directress of such a convent preached, led the women in prayer and may very well have instructed them in mystical wisdom as well. To be sure, though, many ribats, or convents, also served as way stations for widowed or divorced women, a safe haven where they could spend at least the three months and ten days of the *'idda*, the obligatory waiting period, before they were allowed to enter a new marriage. (The commandment to observe the waiting period rests upon Sura 65:4 and was intended to ensure that the woman was not pregnant before she entered into a new marriage.) Very pious women observe the *'idda* at home, passing their time in prayer and meditation and making sure they come in contact with no one outside their most immediate family members. This is still the custom in Pakistan among conservative families today, a fact I was able to witness for myself during my stay in Karachi.

History informs us that the direction of a convent sometimes remained in the family. The granddaughter of the great Sufi Ahmad-i Jam (d. 1146) passed her forty-day confinement in her grandfather's convent, while another woman, Amina Khatun, the granddaughter of the mystical poet Auhaduddin Kirmani, lived and taught in Damascus as a *sheikha* and *hafiza*, "one who knows the Quran by heart."

While remembering them, however, we must not forget the learned female scholars among the Sufis. One of them, Bubu Rasti in Burhanpur in India, was an expert in interpreting medieval Persian mystical texts, especially the interpretation of the works of Fakhruddin 'Iraqi, whose *Lama'at* (Flashes), a small book of poetry mixed with prose, charmingly elucidates several of Ibn ʿArabi's theories and ranks among the finest works we have on mystical love.

Babu Rasti died sometime after 1620, and in the early 1630s the oldest daughter of the Mogul emperor Shah Jahan (ruled 1628–1658), Princess Fatima Jahanara, was initiated into the mystical path along with her younger brother, the heir apparent Dara Shikoh. These royal children were inspired by the saint Mian Mir in Lahore (d. 1635). The heir apparent dedicated a separate chapter in the biography he wrote about this, his mystical teacher, to Mian Mir's own saintly sister, Bibi Jamal Khatun. The princess made such progress along the path that her actual master, Mian Mir's successor Molla Shah (d. 1661), would have named her his successor if the rules of the order would have allowed such a thing. Despite this obstacle, the princess remained true to mysticism, although she had to take on the duties of the First Lady of the Mogul empire in 1631 following the untimely death of her mother (in whose honor the Taj Mahal was erected).

The order into which Fatima Jahanara and her brother had been initiated was the Qadiriyya. In the fourteenth century, this order, founded in the twelfth century in Iraq, was established in the subcontinent, first in southern India and then later in the Punjab. However, the Mogul family usually preferred the Indian Chishtiyya order, and it was in keeping with this tradition that the princess made a pilgrimage to Ajmer after recuperating from severe burns. In this she was following the example set by her great-grandfather Akbar. To this day, Ajmer in Rajastan remains the center of the Chishtiyya order, whose founder, Muʿinuddin Chishti, is buried there. A Persian biography which the princess dedicated to her spiritual leader is preserved in manuscript form in the British Library. After her death in 1681 she was laid to rest in the courtyard of the graceful tomb of Nizamuddin Auliya (d. 1325) in Delhi. As patroness of mystical literature, Jahanara either ordered translations of many works of classical literature or had them explained by commentaries. Her niece Zeb un-Nisa (d. 1689), the daughter of her strictly orthodox brother Aurangzeb (who had Dara Shikoh executed), was also inclined to mysticism and poetry, while the other daughters of the emperor made a name for themselves by giving gifts and alms to the mystics of Delhi.

Other noblewomen in the Islamic world—and not only princesses like Zeb un-Nisa's sister Zinat un-Nisa—are also celebrated as the founders of mosques, for example, in Ahmadabad (Gujarat) and in the Deccan. Even though women are not allowed to enter the inner sanctuaries of many holy places and are compelled to wait at the window and say their prayers while standing there in order to catch a glimpse of the sarcophagus of the saint, they need not have been completely passive or totally excluded from what was going on. There is some evidence they might have greeted the arrival of a holy relic, such as the *hazratbal*, the Noble Hair [of the Prophet] in Bijapur, by chanting litanies. During memorial services at the tomb of Muʿinuddin Chishti, one of his female disciples holds a candle over the heads of all the women assembled in the courtyard, and after this candle is fixed to the grave, even they may enter the tomb. Similar customs are undoubtedly common in many holy places, but we must also recall that several kings (for example, Feroz Shah Tughluq, who reigned from 1351 to 1388 and Sikandar Lodi, who reigned from 1489 to 1517) forbade women to visit the shrine in Ajmer and elsewhere in order to avoid any "unreligious" customs or those not in keeping with the reverence such a site demanded. That there were indeed a number of "nonreligious" customs being practiced near some of the graves of the saints (the most widespread being prostitution) is a fact documented in all the sources, and some sites had a particularly bad reputation in this regard. But there were also places to which even prostitutes would make their pilgrimages in complete reverence.

The various forms of indigenous veneration of pious and saintly women needs more detailed study. One frequently comes across the graves or small tombs of unnamed women, and sources repeatedly mention the "unknown servant of God." In his book about Sindh (1853), even the critical Robert Burton observed that the Sindhis acknowledge "the religious services of the weaker sex." He pays particular attention to one Fatima Hajarani, who had attained the rank of *murshid*, a spiritual guide. People gave romantic names to the graves of such women. In Anatolia, for example, one finds *Pisili Sultan*, "Lady with the cat," and *Karyagdi Sultan*, "Lady 'It snowed,'" to name but two, and in many places there are groups of women like the *Haft ʿafifa*, the "seven chaste ones," who sank into the ground upon the approach of enemy soldiers. People also tell of individual women like those who, confronted by danger, prayed for deliverance, whereupon the earth swallowed them up lest their honor be defiled. Many legends follow the model of Dhu ʿn-Nun's stories by revolving around simple women who serve as examples for others through the strength of their faith. The story of Lalla Mimunah, a simple soul from North Africa, is a very touching tale of this type. Try as she might, she was unable to learn the words of the prayer the captain of a ship was trying to teach her. As the ship left the harbor, she followed behind it, walking on the water in her zeal to finally learn the prayer.

Fatima of Indarpat lived in northern India around 1200 and was said to have been "distinguished by an inner light," and it is said that "her grave is the place to turn with personal requests." This saying is applicable to many other women as well. Fatima's small grave, known to but a very few pious believers, lies in Delhi, not far distant from Nizamuddin Auliya's tomb, and it is visited by Muslim and Hindu women alike.

The Islamic image of pious women dedicated to an ascetic and mystical life is a colorful one, for it includes strict ascetics as well as women scholars, noblewomen who maintained an interest in religious works even in the midst of the duties courtly life imposed upon them, simple girls or old women whose names only vaguely hint at their mystical experiences but who comforted and consoled thousands of women down through the centuries via their *baraka,* their "blessing" or "power of sanctity." These were women to whom the girls and women in town and country turned with their cares in the certain knowledge that they could count on their spiritual help. The image of the saintly woman thus holds a particular significance for Muslim women who frequently turn to their sisters, be they living or long since dead, for comfort and consolation.

➤ 3 · Women in the Quran and in the Tradition ➤

THE QURAN SPEAKS of "pious and believing women," *mu'minat, muslimat,* and even mentions them in the same breath with pious and believing men; moreover, these women are expected to perform the same religious duties as the men are. There is only one negative female figure in the Quran, and she is the wife of Abu Lahab, Muhammad's archenemy. She is mentioned briefly in Sura 111, where she is called "the bearer of faggots." She wears a fiber halter around her neck and serves as an example of the damnation of the unbelievers.

The woman's position as depicted in the Quran is a definite improvement over conditions existing in pre-Islamic Arabia. Women were now able to retain and make their own decisions about the property they either brought with them into or earned during their marriage and were now permitted, for the first time, to inherit. At times, the permission laid down in Sura 4:3 to have four legitimate wives was interpreted as a concession to the four temperaments of man, and yet polygamy is by no means as widespread as is commonly believed. The above-mentioned Quranic rule to the effect that women are to be granted fair treatment has led many modernists to postulate monogamy as the ideal toward which one ought to strive. After all, even if each woman receives the same share of material goods, how could the man possibly harbor the same feelings toward each one of multiple wives? Permission to punish one's wife for repeated disobedience is mitigated by the words of the Prophet recommending the loving treatment of women: "The best among you is he who treats his wife most kindly."

The intimate bond between man and wife is clearly defined in the frequently overlooked or more often than not falsely interpreted words of Sura 2:187: "[Women] are a raiment for you and ye are raiment for them." In religious tradition all over the world, one's garment is one's *alter ego*, that object that is most closely connected with one's personality.

The Quran mentions only one woman by her actual name. This is Mary, the virgin mother of Jesus, who is highly revered in Islam. As one tradition has it, she will be the first to enter paradise. It was for her that the dried up palm tree bore sweet dates as she clung to it during the labors of childbirth, and her newborn infant testified to her purity (Sura 19:24, 30–33). She is the silent, humble soul who would deserve special and extensive study. Although the Quran also speaks of a number of other female figures, some of them and others not mentioned in the Quran were invented by later exegetes or simply created by popular piety. These women were given names and their stories were steadily embellished and elaborated, with the result that they have come to serve as role models for women. An example of one such edifying text is Thanawi's "Paradisiacal Ornament," which didactically presents these Quranic women to the young reader as models suitable for emulation. The very first woman, naturally, is Eve, Hawwa, who, as tradition has it, was created out of Adam's rib. Even Goethe, Germany's greatest poet, was familiar with the Islamic version of this myth. His verse reproduction of this *hadith* admonishes men to treat women with indulgence. Since God took a crooked rib to create her, her resultant form could not be entirely straight. Thus, if man tries to bend her, she will break, and if one leaves her in peace, she only becomes more crooked. The poet then asks Adam, which is to say, man, quite directly: Which is worse? In place of an answer he offers the following advice: treat women with patience and forbearance, for nobody wants a broken rib.[1]

Nowhere does the Quran make Eve responsible for the fall from grace, thus burdening her with having introduced original sin into the world. In fact, Islam does not even recognize the idea of original sin. But in the "Tales of the Prophets," especially in the richly elaborated versions spread by folk preachers and imaginative bards, Eve does play an important role. Her beauty is described in glowing colors: "She was as big and as comely as Adam, had 700 plaits in her hair, was adorned with chrysolite and perfumed with musk. . . . Her skin was more delicate than Adam's and purer in color, and her voice was more beautiful than his."

Tradition also tells how God addressed Adam: "My Mercy I have pulled together for you into My Servant Eve, and there is no other blessing, O Adam, that were greater than a pious wife."

Legends describing the union of the first man with the first woman include all the details that make a worldly wedding so festive, some even going so far as to have angels strew paradisiacal coins over the heads of the bridal couple. But once they succumbed to the temptations of the tiny snake that had entered the garden in the beak of a

[1] Behandelt die Frauen mit Nachsicht!
Aus krummer Rippe ward sie erschaffen,
Gott konnte sie nicht ganz grade machen.
Willst du sie biegen, sie bricht.
Läßt du sie ruhig, sie wird noch krümmer;
Du guter Adam, was ist denn schlimmer?—
Behandelt die Frauen mit Nachsicht:
Es ist nicht gut, daß euch eine Rippe bricht.

peacock, once they had eaten of the forbidden fruit (usually represented as corn), their clothes flew off. Traditional narratives usually take advantage of this passage to emphasize Eve's frivolity. Dramatic descriptions have Eve question God as to where her guilt might lie and what her punishment would be, and God answers: "I shall make you deficient in thought and religion, and in the ability to bear witness and to inherit." These words were culled from two Quranic commandments, according to which two women are needed to bear witness instead of one man (Sura 2:282) and daughters inherit less than sons (Sura 4:11). In the same way, the next divine punishment—"Imprisoned you shall be your whole life long"—developed out of a specific understanding of seclusion that was only intensified over the course of time. According to Kisa'i, Eve was also told that no woman shall "participate in that which is best in life: the common Friday prayers" (even though this prohibition derived neither from the Quran nor from earliest practice). Nor was she supposed to greet anyone, which is another sanction for which there is no Quranic foundation. Her punishments are menstruation and pregnancy, and "a woman shall never be a prophet or a wise man." All of this only goes to show how many widespread assumptions rest *not* upon the words of the Quran but upon rather imaginative interpretations of the same by the believers.

Eve repented of her transgression and was forgiven. But Adam and Eve were separated after their expulsion from Paradise, and, as some legends have it, they met up again only many years later in the vicinity of Mecca. Gabriel was teaching Adam the rites of pilgrimage while he was resting on the hill of Safa. It happens that Eve was on the hill of Marwa at the time (a name imaginative exegetes derived from *mar'a*, "woman"), and they recognized one another, *ta'arafa*, on the plains of 'Arafat.

Abraham's concubine, Hagar, is also associated with pilgrimage. She ran back and forth between Marwa and Safa seven times in order to find water for her thirsty little boy Ismail, and on the seventh trip the spring Zamzam finally bubbled up. This story eventually became the model for the pilgrim's sevenfold "running" between these two hills (which are today connected by an arcade).

Another figure in popular tradition is the daughter of Nimrud, the tyrant who had Abraham tossed onto a burning funeral pyre. The story maintains that this girl, inspired by Abraham's faith, threw herself into the fire as well and, like him, remained untouched by the flames.

Commentators have named Pharaoh's wife, the believer who rescued the baby Moses, Asiya. She soon became the model of a devout woman because she took up and rescued the future prophet despite her husband's precautionary measures. This is how she earned her place in paradise. In fact, certain circles revere her as the "perfect woman" whose beauty, along with that of Mary, Khadija, and Fatima, exceeds the comeliness of all the virgins in Paradise.

There is also another woman in the Quran, the Queen of Saba (Sheba), whom tradition knows as Bilqis. Sura 27 tells how she is first discovered by the hoopoe, *hudhud*, and then follows the call of the prophet king Solomon to accept the true faith and to become his wife. Bilqis was a former sun-worshiper who challenged Solomon with three riddles, which he naturally solved without difficulty. She was so deceived by the reflection of the glass floor in his palace (thinking that she was walking through water) that she tied up her skirts, thus baring her legs (Sura 27:43). It became immediately evident to Solomon that she, the daughter of a jinn (a supernatural spirit) and a mortal woman, had the body of a normal human being. Bilqis's heart clung to her throne, a work of wondrous beauty, and therefore Solomon ordered it miraculously removed to his own palace.

Bilqis frequently turns up in the later literature as the model of a rich, intelligent ruler; thus panegyric poems are fond of mentioning her. The Persian poet Khaqani (d. 1199) praises both the wife and the sister of his patron, the Shir-wan-shah, as Bilqis, just as he frequently uses comparisons with the great women of history, be they Maryam, the mystic Rabiʿa, or Queen Zubaida. In fact, in Khaqani's poems the ladies he eulogizes appear to him to be stronger and better than the men.

Again, the court of the Beloved appears so marvelous in the *Tarjuman al-ashwaq*, the mystically interpreted love poems of the great theosophic mystic Ibn ʿArabi (d. 1240), "that Bilqis could have forgotten her throne" (Nr. XXVI, 3). The beautiful women are described as "peacocks with deadly glances and extraordinary power—one would think that each one of them were a Bilqis on her throne of pearls" (II, 2). And, as Ibn ʿArabi himself explains, he calls divine wisdom "'Bilqis,' for she is the child of 'theory,' which is subtle, and of 'praxis,' which is coarse, just as Bilqis was both spirit and woman since her father was one of the jinns and her mother a mortal being."

For Jami (d. 1492), though, she is the wise queen whose balanced view of good and evil women and gentle criticism of Firdausi's misogynistic verse demonstrate her sagacity. (European literature has a wonderful portrayal of her wise benevolence in Rudyard Kipling's delightful story *The Butterfly that Stamped.*)

Bilqis's throne and references to this powerful queen appear here and there in the lyrical poems as well as in the panegyrics of the Islamic world, and it is not unusual to find the wise queen portrayed in miniature paintings, either sitting on her throne or caught in the moment when the hoopoe tosses Solomon's letter onto her bed. It is all the more surprising, then, that the love between the miracle-working Solomon, who also had the gift of understanding the language of the birds, and the Yemenite queen has not been transformed into a romantic epic as have so many other traditions in Persia. This Quranic story would have been the fitting basis of a wonderful allegory about the spir-

itual power of the divinely inspired ruler and the love of the
unbelieving woman who finds her way to the true faith
through the guidance of his words. Perhaps the poets failed
to find in this tale that tragic element so important to the
other Persian-Turkish epics. As far as I know, Rumi is the
only one who dwelt upon this theme in all its depth and significance. In his *Mathnawi* (M IV, 465ff.) Rumi relates how
Bilqis sent gold to Solomon and how he sent her army back
to her. She then set out on the long journey, during the
course of which she separated herself from the world more
and more every day until her entire being was transformed
into that of the lover (M IV 862):

> Now, as Bilqis set forth with heart and soul,
> she rued the days of old.
> She abandoned both wealth and kingdom
> as lovers forget honor and glory.
> Her gentle maidens and beautiful boys
> seemed to reek of rotting onions,
> and her gardens, palaces and ponds
> appeared as cinders to the eye of love.
> When love overwhelms a person's being,
> all one previously prized suddenly seems odious.
> The emerald is no better than a leek.
> Love's ardor teaches: There is no God but He—
> and He alone! O guardian, 'No God but He'—
> the power of this truth can transform the bright
> moon to a black pot before your very eyes.

In this transformation, Bilqis is rather reminiscent of
Zulaikha, Potiphar's wife in the Old Testament. In the
Islamic tradition, Zulaikha turns into a love-obsessed
woman willing to do anything to attain her beloved Yusuf,
the personification of beauty, whom she passionately
desires:

> Love is like an ocean
> upon which the heavens are mere foam,
> aroused, like Zulaikha, in her love for Yusuf

is the way Rumi put it, the poet who is the best interpreter of this story.

The twelfth Sura of the Quran, whose own words characterize this tale as "the story most beautiful," tells of Yusuf's life, his separation from his father Jacob, the treachery of his brothers; it relates how he was thrown into the pit and then sold to Egypt, how the wife of his master fell in love with him and, reprimanded by all because of her passion, invites all her girlfriends to visit her. When Yusuf enters, they are so enraptured by his appearance that they unconsciously cut their own fingers while peeling the citrus fruits they were preparing. Then follows Yusuf's role in prison, his interpretation of dreams and the high position he ultimately attains, which in turn allows him to sell grain to his brothers during the famine in Canaan. The story ends when Jacob, blinded by weeping for his lost son, is restored to sight by the scent of Yusuf's shirt.

Subsequent literary developments appropriated several scenes from this Quranic narrative and embellished them to the extent that Zulaikha, initially a rather unimportant figure, eventually became the focus of attention.

The Quranic commentators were naturally kindly disposed toward this theme, and it was primarily such mystics as ʿAbdullah-i Ansari of Herat (d. 1089) and his follower Maibudhi who dedicated long and profound explications to the Yusuf story. The theme was probably well known to Iran's poets very early on, even if the tale "Yusuf and Zulaikha," formerly attributed to Firdausi (d. 1020), is no longer recognized as his work, regardless of how diligently nineteenth-century scholars tried to prove its authenticity.

As Hermann Ethé demonstrates, already before the turn of the first millennium Abu ʾl-Muʾayyad al-Balkhi composed an epic about these famous Quranic lovers, and in the course of the centuries innumerable recountings of the material followed, primarily in the eastern Islamic world: Shaukat Bukhari, Amʿaq Bukhari, Nazim-i Harawi, Ruknuddin Harawi are all named in Ethé's list, and the poets in the Indian subcontinent enthusiastically appropriated the theme after Jami of Herat had given it its classic form in a poem that was rendered into German as early as 1824 by Vincenz von Rosenzweig-Schwannau. Mir Ma'sum Nami, the historian and calligrapher from Sind who was associated with Akbar's court, is only one of the many who reworked the theme into Persian verses. Prose works were also written in the Indo-Persian regions, and every one of these versions ends with the happy and detailed depiction of the marriage of Yusuf and Zulaikha. There is a Kashmiri version of the epic, and in Bengali Muhammad Saghir's (d. 1501) rendition of *Yusuf Jalikha* dates back to the fifteenth century. In the Dakhni-Urdu literature of the southern Indian courts several poetic elaborations of the story appear in the seventeenth century, including the one by Malik Khushnud, the court bard of Muhammad 'Adil Shah of Bijapur. In Hashim's poem toward the end of the seventeenth century Zulaikha speaks *rekhti*, the typical woman's idiom of Urdu, and a poet from Gujarat, Mir 'Ali Amin "draped Zulaikha with the robes of respectable ladies," as one critic writes.

Just how many different versions of the Yusuf-Zulaikha-motif appeared in later years in the eastern regions is hard to determine. Naturally the theme was taken up also in Ottoman Turkey, where Hamdi (d. 1503), the son of the mystical leader Aq Shamsuddin, the religious leader of Sultan Mehmet the Conqueror, created one of the most moving renditions of the story. In it, "Zulaikha's Lament" is particularly touching:

> Ever since, when on the day of affirmation
>   [i.e., the Primordial Covenant (Sura 7:172)]
> love sowed the seed of sorrow,
> love let me grow, nourished by the water of pain.
> Then, when pain had threshed out my grains,

love suddenly tossed the harvest to the wind.
Ever since my heart first became acquainted with
  the grief of my Friend,
love estranged all the friends I held dear from me.
Health too bade me farewell, ever since
love stretched out its hand of reprimand
to welcome me.
My eyes have lost all trace of sleep, they overflow
  with tears:
I do not know the destination
love has in store for me.

Certain themes from the story of Yusuf and Zulaikha are repeatedly mentioned and transformed in the epics as well as in countless other references in lyric poetry. One such theme is the auction during which the beautiful slave was supposed to be sold. As everybody gathers around and prepares to bid, a poor old woman with the same intention joins the crowd (see below, p. 70f.). She represents the personification of noble striving which is praiseworthy in itself, even if it fails to attain its goal.

Zulaikha does everything she can think of to seduce Yusuf: she has her palace adorned with sensuous pictures so that Yusuf should see himself and Zulaikha enveloped in the joys of love wherever his eyes may wander. As might be expected, the most detailed depiction of this scene is found in Jami's epic. It is interesting to remember that, more than four hundred years before him, one of the Ghaznavid rulers, Sultan Mas‘ud (d. 1089), ordered a pleasure palace in Jami's hometown of Herat to be decorated with extremely sensuous wall paintings. One almost has the feeling that the memory of such a palace might have somehow subconsciously lived on in Herat. Jami's description understandably inspired the miniature painters of the sixteenth century, for they frequently portrayed a multi-storied palace with the beautiful Yusuf trying to flee over its steep and convoluted steps. Zulaikha appears in these pictures as an attractive woman draped in red robes. (Red was the color of the bridal gown, but it can also be interpreted more generally as an indication of ardent love.) Yusuf, on the other hand, is frequently shown wearing the green garments of the saints, the prophets, and the inhabitants of Paradise.

An interesting aspect of the seduction scene is Zulaikha's attitude toward the idol she keeps in her room; after all, she is still an unbeliever practicing a false religion. She covers the icon to hide her seductive machinations from its view. This scene has to be very old, for the mystic Hujwiri (d. ca. 1071) wrote in his introduction to the *Sufi Path*: "All human beings ought to learn from Zulaikha how to observe good manners in contemplating the object of their adoration, for when she was alone with Joseph and besought him to consent to her wishes, she first covered up the face of her idol in order that it might not witness her want of propriety."[2]

Jami describes the same scene and alludes to it again in another epic poem called *Subhat al-abrar*. Here Yusuf tells her that he is as ashamed before God, the All-Seeing One, as she is before her idol, and he quickly takes his leave.

Jami takes up the theme of the idol once again toward the end of his great poem when the aged Zulaikha begins to doubt that Yusuf will ever turn to her. She smashes the ineffectual statue and, after having thus freed herself from the "idols," and now with the help of the true God, she miraculously attains her goal and is eventually united with her beloved.

This is a fine way to convert to the true faith, but an early mystic, Yusuf ibn Husain ar-Razi (d. 916), has a more profound view: "When she cast desire away, God gave her

---

[2] Ali ibn ʿUsman Hujwiri, *The Kashf al-mahjub: The Oldest Persian Treatise on Sufism, Written by Ali ibn Uthman al-Hujwiri,* trans. Reynold A. Nicholson (London/Leiden, 1911), p. 335.

beauty and youth back to her. It is a law that when the lover advances, the beloved retires. If the lover is satisfied with love alone, then the beloved draws nigh."[3]

Zulaikha thus becomes the woman-soul who lives out her life in harsh repentance and endless longing. "If you are not Zulaikha and are not ground in the mill of love, do not waste time talking of Yusuf of Canaan" is the warning Sana'i, the mystical poet of Ghazna (d. 1131), gives. To his way of thinking, only the one acquainted with the pain of loving Yusuf has any right to speak of love. The poets know that "love tore Zulaikha from the veil of chastity," as Hafiz put it, and she became the symbol for all who suffer the pangs of unrequitable love and longing. She thus became the courageous, strong heroine willing to bear anything for the sake of her Beloved.

"People always looked at Yusuf's torn garment— / But who saw Zulaikha's torn and broken heart?" asked the Indian poet Azad Bilgrami toward the middle of the eighteenth century. The poets describe the woman, once so beautiful, aging in misery and sitting in desperation at side of the road, hoping to catch a glimpse of Yusuf. He, for his part, wants nothing to do with her, as ʿAttar tells in his *Musibatnama*:

> When Jacob set out to visit his son,
> and left Canaan to go to Egypt,
> the Egyptians adorned their land
> from one end to the other.
> When Zulaikha learned of this,
> she threw herself upon the ground, completely
>   overcome.
> She covered her head with a veil
> and crouched humbly by the side of the road.
> As it happened, Yusuf had to pass this spot;
> he saw the sad and afflicted one.

[3] Ibid., p. 136.

High on his horse, with whip in hand,
he struck the woman so morbidly in love
    with him.
A sigh rang out from the depths of her heart,
whose ardor the cane but whipped to flame,
and, as the fire grew ever stronger,
Yusuf, most miserable, dropped his whip.
Zulaikha said: "O thou with faith so pure—
is it too much for you, that you can't bear it!
This flame has sprung from out my heart
and you can't hold it in your hand?
The flame that has filled me for years—
can you not hold it for even a moment?
You, of all Believers the First—and I a woman!
Is that how you show your fidelity?"

Like Jacob, Zulaikha, too, turns blind from constant weeping and yearns only for a passing scent of Yusuf's presence. Hujwiri says: "Since Zulaikha was ready to die on account of her excessive love for Yusuf, her eyes were not opened until she was united with him."

Only the thought of Yusuf kept her alive; she thinks exclusively of his name just as the soul should constantly think of the Divine Beloved. Thus Ibn ʿArabi relates in his *Futuhat al-makkiyya* (II 375): "It was said that Zulaikha was once wounded by an arrow. As her blood dripped to the ground, it traced out the name 'Yusuf, Yusuf' wherever it landed; because she so constantly repeated this name, it flowed like blood in her veins."

This image had already been employed in early Sufism, where it is told that a Sufi's blood kept on writing the word "Allah" in the dust after he had been accidentally injured. Ibn ʿArabi, however, used the example of Zulaikha when mentioning how the blood of the martyr-mystic Hallaj also wrote the name of God.

After this period of yearning and desperation, Zulaikha's unshakable fidelity is finally rewarded. "Be patient like

Zulaikha," Sana'i never tires of teaching his readers, for he knows that the mere proximity of the beloved has rejuvenating powers: "When the torments of your lower soul and the weakness of your body have rendered you old and shabby, rejuvenate your soul, like Zulaikha, by yearning for your Friend."

'Attar, who belongs to the next generation of mystical poets, describes this rejuvenation in a dramatically moving scene in his *Ilahinama:*[4]

> One day Joseph the Pure was walking along when he saw Zulaikha seated on the ground;
> The world hidden from her eyes, but then she had averted her eyes from the world;
> Afflicted with sickness and poverty, beside herself in a hundred different ways;
> Every moment suffering more than a hundred griefs, more concerned about Joseph than Joseph himself;
> Sitting on the road as though hoping that she might receive some of the dust raised by his feet;
> That perhaps some dust might rise from the road traveled by that king-like one.
> When Joseph saw her he said: "O God, what wilt Thou with this blind and decrepit old woman?
> Why doest Thou not cause her to disappear seeing that she sought to bring disgrace on Thy prophet?"
> Gabriel descended and said: "We shall not remove her,
> For she has within her a whole world of love for him whom We love.
> Since her love for thee is unceasing I too love her for thy sake.
> Who told thee to seek the death of the rose in the garden and to wish for the destruction of the friends of Our friends?
> Though for a lifetime I have driven her to despair yet I

---

[4] Quoted from *The Ilahi-nama or Book of God of Farid al-Din 'Attar,* translated from the Persian by John Andrew Boyle, with foreword by Annemarie Schimmel (Manchester, 1976), p. 297f.

will now make her young again for thee.

She has given thee her own precious soul; if I now bless
her let her be to thee as thy soul.

Since she is filled with tenderness for Our Joseph, who
would think in hatred of taking her life?

If she claims to love such a king as thou, her weeping
eyes bear witness to her love."—

Since this lover has her witnesses with her her glory
increases more and more every day.

Thus the loving Zulaikha comes to personify the human
soul, the *nafs*, which, as the Quran says in Sura Yusuf,
"incites to evil, *ammara biʾs-su*," but which is purified
through constant inner struggle and suffering and can
finally return to her Lord as "the soul at peace." The scent
of Yusuf's shirt touches her and reveals his beauty, for
scent, the breath of the Merciful One, brings news of the
beloved, and the proximity of the beloved rejuvenates the
woman ravaged by grief. Jami and the poets who followed
his model describe in great detail the wedding of the couple,
now finally united. Zulaikha, once betrothed to an impotent
husband, is still a virgin, and now the loving Yusuf tears
the garment from his chaste bride as she had once torn his
shirt from him. All of this, though, has little to do with the
profoundly mystical content of the story, which is itself a
perfect illustration of the primordial interplay of Beauty
and Love as Jami so aptly expressed it in the introduction
to his epic poem.

4 · Woman or "Man of God": The Education of the Soul (*nafs*)

ZULAIKHA THE SEDUCTRESS—that's the way she appears in the Quran—and for those who lived in ascetic fear of the feminine it must have been very gratifying that exactly the Sura Yusuf, which denounces such seductive arts, talks of the *nafs*, the "soul," in terms of its being *ammara bi's-su,* "inciting to evil" (Sura 12:53). Wasn't the grammatical gender of the very word *nafs* feminine? Couldn't it therefore serve as a symbol for the woman whose sensuality always thwarts the religious inclinations, the high-minded strivings of the rationally oriented man? Since she possesses more animalistic traits than does the man, she constantly tries to seduce him through her sexual wiles.

Every culture prefers boys to girls: familiar to all are the rites with which the birth of a boy is greeted with joy whereas the birth of a girl is noted with disappointment. This explains why some Muslim saints have been credited with miracles transforming newborn girls into boys. . . . The fear of women, who, as the Prophet is supposed to have said, "can overcome the rational ones," is reflected in numerous sayings and tales from the early years of Islam. "The woman is evil through and through, and the most evil thing about her is that she is absolutely necessary!" This remark has been attributed to ʿAli ibn Abi Talib, who, as the husband of the Prophet's daughter Fatima, actually

69

ought to have had a more positive attitude. And yet, always supposing the statement did indeed stem from him, these words were probably uttered during the thirty years after Fatima's death, which is to say, when he had had a number of subsequent wives.

If Sura 12:53 speaks of the *nafs* as "inciting to evil," then the same concept, i.e., *nafs*, but qualified by different adjectives, can be found also in two other places in the Quran, namely: where it speaks of the *nafs lawwama*, the "accusing soul" (Sura 75:2), and the *nafs mutma'inna*, the "soul at peace" (Sura 89:27). As the latter the soul can return, "pacified and pacifying," to its Lord. Apart from these three specific references, however, the word is value-free in the Quran and refers for the most part to the "self" in a very general sense.

The three Quranic verses cited above offered the Sufis an excellent incentive to resist and to rear their instinctual drives to the point where they could slowly hope to attain the highest stage of perfection. Didn't the Prophet say that man's worst enemy was the *nafs*, and that the struggle against it was the "greatest *jihad*"?

In its absolute sense the word *nafs* is used in religious texts almost exclusively to denote the "base instincts," the evil qualities of man. The countless allegories that speak of the "taming of the shrew," of the necessary harsh education of the *nafs*, are to be understood in this way. One of its most important manifestations, however, is in the form of woman. This feminine element, then, is subordinate to the *'aql*, the intellect or reason, which has as its task to tame and train it. Thus, the *nafs* appears in many texts, and primarily in Rumi's *Mathnawi*, as the mother of mankind, whereas *'aql* appears as the father. In Rumi's verses we find very realistic descriptions of marital strife, during the course of which the soft-hearted mother argues that her tender little boy really shouldn't go to school, but rather be left to her care to be spoiled, whereas Father Intellect wants to give the child a good education and thus wants to send him off to a strict school so that he might progress along the path of perfection (M VI 1433ff.).

The *nafs* can also appear as the foster mother of humankind and is occasionally depicted along its developmental path, which includes the stage of *nafs lawwama*, which is to say, the accusing, self-reproaching soul, which slowly succumbs to her husband without ever being entirely certain of his love.

Actually, Rumi's very first tale in the *Mathnawi* (M I, 36-245) tells of a lovesick slave girl, and it can be interpreted as an allegory about the weaning of the base instincts from the "world." As the physician (who is meant to represent the First Intellect) determines, the sick girl is in love with a goldsmith (symbol of the seductive material world), and the physician cures her by letting the unworthy object of her love gradually deteriorate until she finally turns away from it and toward the actual object of her love, the king.

Just about all the heroines of the mystical tales and epic poems are, in the end, *nafs* figures, for this metaphor expresses the potential that women can attain to a higher stage of perfection and that each one of these initially unworthy figures can become a true "man of God," which is to say, that she can reach her goal of becoming "a soul at peace." Women like Bilqis and Zulaikha are celebrated as often as they are in the classical literature of the Islamic world because they fulfill this very function—a function the love stories of Indian Islam (see below, pp. 102ff.) expanded on in even greater detail.

As every individual woman can be looked upon as the personification of the *nafs* and thus can be despised and scorned by the "men of God," so too can the world, *dunya* (whose grammatical gender just happens to be feminine, as well) be represented as a woman. Like medieval European Christian writers, Sufis too were acquainted with "Mistress World," an abominable old slut who seduces unsuspecting stupid men with her outward beauty only to swallow them up or turn her worm-infested back on them, or to reveal her disgusting varicose-veined legs after she has attained her goal. Medieval texts are a rich source of such images, and they often leave little to be desired as far as black humor is concerned.

"Who is this shabby old hag? An unappetizing hypocrite, layer upon layer like a little onion, as malodorous as a little garlic!" (D 2776). These are the words of Rumi, who also amusingly relates the machinations of this monster in the sixth book of his *Mathnawi.* In an attempt to hide her wrinkles, she goes so far as to tear up a precious illuminated copy of the Quran. This in itself is a particular sacrilege, since the Quran must be treated with the greatest respect at all times and may not be mishandled in any way. She then glues the glittering tatters over her wrinkles in order to appear elegant (M VI 1222–36, 1268–82)! Similarly, a Panjabi Sufi poet of the nineteenth century described the duplicitous "world" as *bangalam,* a "bengali sorceress" who incites everyone to fruitless activity through the magical melodies of her flute.

Sometimes, though, an ascetic can actually employ his spiritual powers to the point of making this hag serve his own purposes, since the one who is obedient to God also enjoys the obedience of all others (and this includes the world, as well).

Of course, one must be ever mindful of the wise words of Yahya ibn Muʿadh (d. 871), who said: "The man of the world adorns the world as if she were a bride; the ascetic blackens her face and pulls her hair out; but the one who loves God ignores her completely." Even if one were to struggle against the world, it would still mean taking a certain interest in it, and such an interest, albeit negative, is already a deviation from the actual goal of the religious path.

The motif of "Mistress World" is often applied in a very specific context: the soul, likened to a highborn falcon, falls into the hands of a cunning old woman. The ancient myth of the fall of the soul into the world of material goods or into exile is a particularly popular image among Persian poets, for falconry still remains a popular sport in the entire Middle East. The old woman incarcerates the poor bird, sews its eyes shut or covers it head with a hood. As a result, the noble bird forgets its origins, the homeland where it was accustomed to live in freedom and where it was borne aloft on the hand of its ruler. Suhrawardi, the Master of Illumination (d. 1191), told this allegory in his prose work, and Rumi, who was particularly fond of the bird motif, described the suffering of this falcon soul at the hands of the old woman in one chapter of his *Mathnawi* (M IV 2557) in somewhat amusing images. She tries to raise it according to her own ideals, thus trimming its wings and talons and feeding it things it finds both despicable and indigestible. When it refuses to eat the wonderful noodle soup she places before it, she suddenly pours the boiling broth over its head: "Ach, the filthy old woman / really means well!" Rumi mocks. For how could "Mistress World" have even the slightest idea of the needs of a bird-soul?

Such negative images of the feminine are a familiar aspect of all religious movements marked by an ascetic strain, and this holds as true for Christian theology as it does for the teachings of the Buddha. The ascetic's fear of *shahwa*, "lust" or "desire," gave rise to the idea that "woman's companionship gnaws away at the roots of life." This attitude led to a trend toward celibacy among the early Sufis, and surely even more ascetics would have preferred celibacy if it had not been for the venerable custom, the *sunna* of the Prophet, to marry. There are a number of tales that tell how the Prophet appeared to this or that ascetic in his dreams and admonished him to follow his noble example and marry so that he might become a true member of his community. Many followed this admonition; yet the general attitude of the ascetics seems to have been best expressed in the statement attributed to Ibrahim ibn Adham (d. ca. 777): "When a man marries, he boards a ship, and when a child is born unto him, he suffers shipwreck."

Even a mystic as happily married as Maulana Rumi has made very negative remarks about marriage. In chapter 17 of his *Fihi ma fihi,* Rumi writes that women exist solely as a prop with which to perfect oneself. In practicing patient tolerance of her absurd ideas, one purifies oneself in rather the same way one uses a towel to wipe dirt away. The struggle and the constant self-denial that married life demands were best left to the strong, and whoever did not feel himself equal to the task was better advised to follow the example of Jesus, who chose the path of celibacy and homelessness.

Rumi is also the author of one of the most dramatic descriptions of a Sufi marriage we have (even though we know that many such marriages seem to have been happy enough when both partners were equally interested in the religious life and the wife was one of the "Friends of God"). In his *Mathnawi* (M VI 2044ff.), Rumi tells how a disciple wanted to visit the great sheikh Kharaqani (d. 1034), but, after having heard so many negative things from the latter's wife about her useless, stupid husband, he returned to the forest, completely disillusioned and disheartened. There he happened to run into the master riding a lion and brandishing a snake as a whip. Kharaqani told the incredulous visitor that this was his divine reward for having demonstrated so much patience toward his insufferable wife.

For many Sufis, marriage could actually serve as a foretaste of hell or at least as a substitute for the punishments one could expect to meet there. Since Jonas, we are told, wanted to experience his share of hell's retribution, he was encouraged to marry a certain woman, for "your punishment is the daughter of so-and-so. Marry her." Indeed, Malik ibn Dinar felt that a man should leave his wife in order to devote himself exclusively to God, and some other

Sufi said: "If God is favorably disposed toward one of His servants, He lets his wife die and grants him [the opportunity] of dedicating himself totally to the worship of God." Of course, now and again an evil woman could be converted to the true faith by one of her husband's miracles, for instance, his miraculously providing food or sustenance for her or other people.

In light of the overwhelming number of negative remarks about wives, it is all the more refreshing to come across a remark like the one made by the Delhi mystic Mir Dard (d. 1785), who writes: "I love my wife and children beyond measure and am completely absorbed in my love for my wife and child. God knows whether that's a result of animal instincts or is part of my human nature or stems from purely sensuous love or is the reflection of Divine Sovereignty in its aspect as the Merciful One. . . ." How far removed from the attitudes of the strict ascetics who considered it a sin to stroke a child, even to kiss their own children, for such acts struck them as a diversion from the true concentration of all love on God alone. Rumi—speaking of one of those ascetics—put it this way: : "The death of his children was sweetmeat to him" (an attitude, by the way, that one finds among the Christian saints as well, including Catherine of Genoa).

And yet Sahl at-Tustari (d. 896) was already emphasizing the importance of conjugal love during Islam's early period. "Love for your wife, in so far as it includes affection and tenderness, need not exclude your love for God—," and for every bite the husband lovingly places in his wife's mouth, he will receive a divine reward. Later on, especially in the succession of Ibn ʿArabi, several mystics expanded even further upon thoughts like these, a point made clear by Sachiko Murata in her highly informative article on the subject.

Of course, only the chosen ones could fully enact the mysteries of marriage as they were experienced by the

Prophet, just as they alone could achieve complete submersion in the Divine during the act of sexual union.

Popular Muslim tradition traced the idea that the woman is incomplete—"deficient in reason and religion" as both medieval Christian and medieval Islamic theology was fond of saying—back to the role of Eve and the way the "Tales of the Prophets" depicted it (see above, pp. 41ff.). These ideas have no Quranic foundation. It was exacerbated by the fact that women were not allowed to touch or recite from the Quran during their days of impurity—a special interpretation of the Quranic commandment "Only the purified may touch it" (Sura 56:79). But Rumi knew that God also hears the prayers of menstruating women (M II 1798-99). Ideas like this, which looked upon the woman, upon whom the Quran calls to fulfill all religious obligations, as something of low and dangerous qualities, ultimately led to the habit of calling anyone who truly walked along God's path a "man." An Arabic saying that originated in thirteenth-century northern India is very clear on this point: *Talib al-maula mudhakkar . . .* , "Whoever seeks the Lord is a male, whoever seeks the otherworld is a passive pederast, whoever seeks the world is a female."

This is the way the Sufis spread their ideal of the "man," and it is typical that works such as the thirteenth-century Arabic text by the Moroccan at-Tadili bear the title *At-tashawwuf fi rijal at-tasawwuf,* "Looking Upon the *Men* of Sufism." However, almost more important than the concept of *rajul,* "man," is the concept of *fata,* the heroic youth who possesses all positive traits. The Quran uses the word *fata* to describe Abraham (Sura 21:60) and, in the plural form, to describe the Seven Sleepers (Sura 18:10). According to tradition, though, ʿAli ibn Abi Talib is the actual *fata* and is portrayed as such in thousands of inscriptions on weapons and vessels: "There is no *fata* like ʿAli and no sword except (ʿAli's two-edged) Dhu ʾl-fiqar." Turkish uses the word *er* or *eren* to denote the true man of God, and Persian poetry is full of praise for the *mard*, the "genuine man." Thus, it's not hard to see how the great Ismaili poet-philosopher Nasir-i Khusrau (d. after 1072) could state that the Prophet was the only true man, while all others are but "women." And yet the mystics were well aware that a woman who walked along the path of God was no woman, but rather a "man," which is the way they first described Rabi'a. Moreover, when in the tradition of the early Indian Chishti order Fatima of Indarpat, a woman distinguished for her great piety and high spiritual gifts, was described as "a man who was sent to earth in the physical form of a woman," what we have is but another manifestation of the same idea. Nizamuddin Auliya (d. 1325), another representative of this tradition, advised the dervishes seeking the intercession of the saints to turn first "to the saintly women because they are rarer."

According to Ibn 'Arabi, true *rajuliyya*, "manliness," is perfected and complete "when the man is purified by the light of the intellect and of spiritual guidance, after he has left the darkness of nature and base desires behind him."

On the other hand, men who are unable to meet the demands of the path of God are considered worse and lower than "women." Such ideas are probably well known in most Sufi traditions, whether in India, Iran, or Turkey. For, as 'Attar says in his *Musibatnama*, "He who is not pregnant from the pain of love / He is a woman, he is not a man." This couplet takes advantage of the common Persian rhyme of *mard*, "man," with *dard*, "pain."

And if many alleged saints boasted of their miracles, the truly pious ones might state: "miracles are the menstruation of men." By this they meant that, by taking pride in certain miraculous deeds, these mystics sank to the low level of females, who, as a result of their impurity, do not attain the union they so ardently desire.

For the true believer, there is no difference between a man and a woman as far as God's love is concerned. A

Persian verse echoes an old proverb when it says:

> Not every woman is a woman,
> not every man a man;
> God did not make identical
> the fingers of one hand.

The Turkish Sufis express this idea with the proverb: *erkek arslan da arslan, disi arslan arslan degilmi?* "A male lion is a lion. Is that to say that a female lion is not a lion as well?" This expression was very popular among the Indian Sufis as early as 1300. When speaking of pious women, Nizamuddin Auliya used to say: "When a wild lion leaves the jungle and enters an inhabited area, no one asks: 'Is it male or female?' for all the children of Adam, men as well as women, are called to piety and to the service of God."

Ibn ʿArabi wrote along the same lines in his *Futuhat al-makkiyya*: "Everything we said of these people under the name of 'men' also applies to the women among them." The fact that a woman might act as a teacher of the mystical path can be gleaned—if in a somewhat coded way—from Rumi's tale about the chickpeas (M IV 4158ff.). Here it is the housewife who teaches the peas the secret of "dying and becoming," of sacrifice and metamorphosis.

It was Jami who described Rabiʿa in this tradition as a creature existing beyond the distinctions of biological gender. In his hagiographic work *Nafahat al-uns*, he writes:

> If all women were like the one we have mentioned,
> then women would be preferred to men.
> For the feminine gender is no shame for the sun,
> nor is the masculine gender an honor for the moon.[1]

Jami employs the same image to describe a pious woman who had renounced her money, her property, and her marital state; as he relates in his *Subhat al-abrar*, there is "a

---

[1] Quoted from Annemarie Schimmel, *Mystical Dimensions of Islam* (Chapel Hill, N.C., 1975), p. 435.

'man'-like woman in Mosul, a lioness, who is not deceived by foxes."

Yet perhaps the most beautiful description of such a pious woman whose worth lies beyond the differentiating characteristics of physical gender is to be found in his epic *Silsilat adh-dhahab*. In this poem Jami sings of a heroic woman ascetic in Egypt—the same one, by the way, whom he had already mentioned briefly in his hagiography after learning about her from Yafi'i. This poem tells how she persisted, motionless, in her meditation:

> Almost thirty years she stood in space
> and, like a tree, never moved from the spot.
> Birds fell quietly to sleep on her head
> while snakes formed anklets around her legs.
> The rain washed her hair
> while the morning breezes daily combed it.
> The only protection she had against the sun
> that parched the earth was the rare cloud above.
> Her mouth refused both food and drink,
> for, like an angel, she partook of no meal.
> Everywhere grasshoppers and ants,
> even wild beasts, encircled her.
> She stood in their midst, confused, bewildered—
> was she alive? or had she experienced total
>   de-becoming?
> Her eye rested on the One Sole Beauty.
> Her soul submerged in the flood of love.
> Her heart rose high in spiritual flights,
> while into her ear profound mysteries penetrated.
> Don't call her a "woman"—for even one strand
>   of her hair
> is still better than a hundred men.

That means, the concepts "man" and "woman" are earthly, bound to the ephemeral form made of dust, whereas the soul has nothing to do with dust. When man and woman have finally attained the state of complete "de-becoming" they no longer have an individual existence any more, as ʿAttar had already explained in his hagiography. This is why Jami concludes his hymn to the nameless female Egyptian ascetic with the prayer that, in the world of oneness, God should keep him from perceiving even the slightest differences between man and woman—a prayer that would surely find resonance in every truly pious person's heart and mind.

⌐ 5 · The Old Woman ⌐───────

EVEN THOUGH the dangerous and loathsome Mistress World is frequently and popularly represented as an old hag, the theme of the "old woman" (sometimes also that of the weak widow) has yet another, positive significance in the Islamic tradition. The Quranic injunction to honor one's parents and to assist the poor and the orphaned (Sura 2:215), together with the traditional respect for older people, all led to the special position accorded the old woman. The charming story of the wrinkled old lady who asked the Prophet whether bleary-eyed old women would ever enter Paradise has been mentioned above; she sighed in distress when the Prophet said no, but cheered up again upon hearing his smiling response: "No, bleary-eyed old women do not go to heaven; they are all transformed into beautiful virgins." Later on, the "faith of the old women of the community" was just another way of describing the way simple souls unquestioningly accepted revealed truths. This ideal faith was contrasted to the hair-splitting arguments of the scholastic theologians or philosophers. In modern times, of course, it can also describe the attitude of those conservative circles that cling to outdated traditions and refuse to adjust to modern life. Such conservative adherence to their "old wives' tales" actually hinders any real progress.

Such thoughts about progress, however, belong to a later era than the one we are talking about. In his "Tales of the Prophets," Kisaʾi tells the story of an old woman who tries to buy an idolatrous icon from Abraham. This prophet, who had already smashed his father's idols, refuses and converts her to belief in the One God instead. Later on, the strength of her new faith miraculously healed the wounds she suffered when, upon orders of the tyrannical Nimrod, her hands and feet were cut off. The image of the old woman or the poor widow appears in the mystical literature even earlier than this, though. The Egyptian mystic Dhu ʾn-Nun (d. 859) tended to make poor, common people the bearers of religious truth, and among these he particularly liked to include old women. "During his journey an old woman asked him who he was, and he answered: 'I am a stranger!' She then asked: 'Is there any such thing as a stranger when one is with God?'"

Yafiʿi (d. 1367) passes on a related tale about ʿAbduʾl Wahid ibn Zayd (d. 794), one of the very first of the known ascetics. On his way to Jerusalem, the latter was accompanied by a woman, who told him: "How can someone who knows Him be a stranger?" She hurried away, saying "my path is the path of the knower. The ascetic is someone who walks, the knower is one who flies."

Even more beautiful is the famous tale in which Dhu ʾn-Nun asks an unnamed old woman: "'What is the end of love?' She responded: 'Love has no end.' And I asked: 'Why?' She answered: 'You idiot! Because the Beloved has no end.'"

Here the woman appears as someone who knows the secret of love. Since God, the Eternal and Unending One, has neither boundaries nor end, the love that man feels for Him can have no end, either. This one sentence summarizes the entire message behind the later mystical love poetry. The extraordinary older women whom Ibn ʿArabi met in his youth in Sevilla appear to be personifications of such wonderful, wise, legendary figures.

Sufism is also well aware of the widow's mite. Legend has it that the great master of the Suhrawardiyya order, Abu Hafs ʿUmar as-Suhrawardi (d. 1234), received rich gifts upon his return from the pilgrimage, but the one he most treasured was the small coin a little old woman had given him along the way.

Of course, legends also tell of an old woman who was able to pluck money out of the clear blue sky just as Rabiʿa was said to have done at one time.

The old women of these tales also know the pain of love. ʿAttar gives a clear indication of this when, during his description of the stoning of Hallaj, he lets an old woman in the crowd fire up the others with her cries: "Hit him hard, teach this woolcarder that it hurts to speak lovingly with God!"

ʿAttar erected a fine monument in his *Ilahinama* to an old woman who was consumed by the ardor of her love for God: whoever burns with love for God has no fear of the physical flame that reduces a house to ashes and soot:

> One day in the market of Baghdad there broke out an extremely destructive fire.
>
> At once a cry arose from the people; a tumult emerged out of that fire.
>
> A poor afflicted old woman, staff in hand, came along the road from some direction.
>
> Someone said to her: "Go on further, thou art mad; the fire has reached thy house."
>
> The woman answered: "It is thou who art mad, hold thy peace, for God will never burn my house."
>
> Finally, when the fire had consumed a whole world of houses, it was found that the old woman's house had remained unscathed.
>
> They said to her: "Tell us, good woman, how wast thou aware of such a mystery?"

The old woman humbly answered: "God could burn
either my house or my heart.

Since He had already burnt my poor crazy heart with
grief He would not burn my house also."[1]

The old woman or widow, however, has still another
important function, one that appears mainly in Persian
epic poetry. In his *Hadiqat al-haqiqa* (The Garden of Truth),
Sanaʾi tells of the poor widow who complained to the
mighty Sultan Mahmud of Ghazna (ruled 999–1030) that
five of his Turkish soldiers had plundered her vineyard.
Mahmud immediately ordered the five evildoers hanged in
order to demonstrate how deeply concerned he was about
justice and caring for the old and the indigent.

Nizami (d. 1209) tells a similar story in his *Makhzan al-
asrar*, albeit transposing the identity of the ruler to the
Seljuk Sanjar (d. 1157), a figure closer to him in both time
and space. Jami (d. 1492) then absorbed the tale whole
cloth, as it were, into his *Silsilat adh-dhahab*, the "Golden
Chain." In this version, too, the monarch is impressed by
the woman's fearlessness, for she places herself directly in
front of his approaching horse and openly accuses his soldiers of robbing her of her laboriously tended grapes. The
result was that

> He gave her gold and a vineyard as well,
> so that her children could eat of its fruit.

The scene of a bent, grieving old woman standing before a
proud horseman with petition in hand is a frequent one in
Persian miniatures. Taken out of context and viewed
absolutely, she could likewise be interpreted as the aged
Zulaikha standing before the beautiful and radiant hero
Yusuf.

---

[1] *The Ilahi-nama or Book of God of Farid al-Din ʿAttar*, translated from
the Persian by John Andrew Boyle, with foreword by Annemarie Schimmel
(Manchester, 1976), p. 142f.

The theme of the old woman as admonisher or warning voice turns up in another context as well. Once again it is ʿAttar, who, in his *Ilahinama*, tells of the old woman who appeared to the mighty Mahmud of Ghazna in a dream after he had studiously ignored her during the day when she tried to give him her petition. The story goes on to tell how she eventually saved humanity. Even if the poem does boil down to a glorification of the mighty king, the oppressed woman is still the focus of attention in the story. Her prayer is the source of help:

> The Sultan of the Faith, Mahmud the Conqueror, was riding swiftly on his Arab horse at the head of his army.
> Somewhere on the roadside he saw a widow who had fastened a petition on the end of a staff.
> She sued for justice against the tyrannous and sought help of that help-giver.
> When the mighty king saw that old woman he paid her no attention but hurried on his way.
> That night Mahmud dreamt that he had fallen into the whirling waters of a well.
> That same old woman appeared and turned her staff round for him.
> She said to him: "Lay hold, O king, and rise from the bottom of this whirlpool and well."
> The king caught hold of the old woman's staff and so escaped with ease from that well of calamity.
> The next day he was sitting on his throne, heavy of heart because of his dream of the night before,
> When again he saw the forlorn old woman approaching from afar to seek justice,
> With staff in hand and bowed of back, her eye moist as a cloud from weeping.
> The king leapt up and called her to sit down beside him.
> Then he said to his troops: "Had it not been for her, last night the crocodile of death would have carried me off.
> By giving me her staff to hang upon she saved me from the whirlpool and the well.
> If you too wish today to have victory from God for ever,

All of you lay hold of her staff, for that will support you always."

The soldiers fell over one another as they rushed forward and took firm hold of that staff.

And all the time great crowds came in from every side to touch the staff.

Whilst the old woman sat on the throne beside the king holding that staff in her hand,

And holding it out as a support for which many eagerly vied with one another.

Like Moses she drew strength from that staff which wrought for the Faith like the staff of Moses.

The king said to her: "O poor old woman, thou art very feeble and there are so many people.

Weak as thou art, how canst thou with a piece of wood support so great a burden?

Many are pulling against you. Thou canst not carry all of this load."

The old woman opened her mouth and said: "O king, whoever can pull Mahmud out of a well can support the weight of anyone. Thy words cannot be admitted.

Whoever can pull an elephant out of a well, how should he hold back from a handful of gnats?"[2]

The piety and unshakable faith of the old woman are stronger than the strongest obstacles, mightier than the mightiest prince on earth.

The image of the loving old woman appears in yet another situation, which once again underscores her role as the personification of the longing soul. Legend has it that, during the auctioning of Yusuf in Egypt, all those present bid extraordinarily high sums in order to acquire the radiantly beautiful prisoner for their own. But, as ʿAttar tells us in *Mantiq ut-tair*, an old woman insinuated herself into the crowd of bidders:

[2] Ibid., p. 135f.

> A wizened old woman joined the crowd:
> "Hey, let me buy this man so proud!"
> Thus shouting to the broker she said
> while in her hand she carried some thread.
> "His form and beauty are driving me wild—
> see all this thread on spools I've filed!
> Take it as payment and sell him to me.
> And place his hand in mine, gently."
> The merchant smiled and said, "Simple soul,
> I've already got bids worth a hundredfold;
> this pearl among jewels is not for you.
> Old woman, what can I with your threads do?"
> "I know I'll never gain this treasure
> but friend and foe will do me pleasure
> to tell the world, although so sly,
> at least she wasn't afraid to try!"

Here we have an example of *himmat*, honorable high ambition; the old woman knows she can never attain her goal, but that doesn't keep her from trying to get as close as possible. The intention is what counts, for it serves as the measure of a person's deeds. This is the sense in which the early-sixteenth-century Turkish poetess Hubba equates the seeker's prayer with the old woman's thread:

> Everyone gives whatever he's got
> If only to share in everyone's lot.
> You and the old woman are alike in this:
> What did she offer for Yusuf's bliss?
> She came with both hands full of thread
> In hopes of buying that beautiful head.

The message here is clear: however bleak the prospect that one's prayers might be heard or answered, one should not give up—the true secret of the search lies in the very hope and confidence that motivate the soul to strive for the highest goal in the first place. If a soul seeks God as ardently as the old woman in the story seeks Joseph, miraculous things can come of the search. It can happen, for instance, that, during her pilgrimage, the seeker will no longer circumambulate the Kaaba, but the Kaaba itself will circle around her, as Sahl al-Tustari (d. 896) learned from an old woman in Mecca, who told him: "The one who journeys beyond selfhood to gaze at the beauty of God—the Kaaba itself will encircle him!"

— 6 · The Mothers —

THE QURAN EXHORTS BELIEVERS to honor their parents as long as they live (Sura 17:23). But the sayings of the Prophet emphasize a person's duties toward his or her parents even more strongly: "Be good to your parents, for only then will your children be good to you, and be yourselves chaste, for then your wives will be chaste."

Although both parents are to be honored and respected, the mother is the one on whom her children should lavish their love, for "paradise lies at the feet of the mothers." According to one tale, a youth came to the Prophet and asked: "Who is most deserving of my love and care?" The Prophet answered: "Your mother!" "And the next most deserving?" "Your mother!" "And the third?" The Prophet replied: "Your mother!" And Rumi's *Mathnawi* (M VI, 3257) reminds us: "[Since] a mother's tenderness derives from God, it's a sacred duty and a worthy task to serve her."[1]

It is not surprising that mothers play a very special role in the biographies of great scholars and saintly men. After all, the child was raised in the women's part of the house under the care and keeping of his mother and aunts during

---

[1] *The Mathnawi of Jalaluddin Rumi*, edited from the Oldest Manuscripts, with Critical Notes, Translation and Commentary by Reynold A. Nicholson (London, 1925; reprint, E. J. W. Gibb Memorial Series, New Series [n.p.], 1968), p. 438.

the first seven years of his life. It was only natural, then, that he should absorb his mother's piety. Books that were meant to serve as guides in raising young girls, such as Thanawi's "Paradisiacal Ornament," tell of many mothers (and sisters) of great scholars of the early period of Sufism who spent their whole fortune on a good education for their sons (and brothers). One example is the great scholar Bukhari (d. 870), to whom Muslims owe the most widely accepted collection of *hadith*. In later years, this sometimes gave rise to the conviction that girls had a certain moral obligation to relinquish their fortunes for their brothers, which was, of course, a perversion of the originally voluntary good deed.

How many pious men carried their fragile mothers to Mecca so that they could complete their pilgrimage! The miracles they performed include the healing of a blind or sick mother. On the other hand, the mother's prayers were particularly effective and could even bring back a captured or otherwise lost son.

The biographies tell us that there were learned and active women among the mothers of the pious. One such woman was the mother of Majduddin Baghdadi (d. 1209), herself a successful physician, who tried to soften her son's harsh novitiate in a Sufi convent. When she learned the boy had been ordered to clean the latrines, she sent twelve Turkish slaves to do the task in his stead. The master sent them back with the remark: "You are a physician—if somebody comes to you with gall bladder complaints, is *he* the one who has to take the medicine or do you give it to a Turkish slave?" There seem to have been a considerable number of good women physicians back then, just as there were women who produced the medicines, the eye salves, and similar remedies. In fact, sons could even be named after an extraordinary mother, as was Ibn Bibi, a thirteenth-century writer in Anatolia, whose learned mother Bibi was called *al-munajjima*, "the [female] astronomer (or astrologer)."

Other women served as models for their sons through their exemplary ascetic lives. Famous in this respect is the mother of the ascetic Ibn Khafif (d. 982) in Shiraz. As a youth he used to castigate himself with almost super-human bouts of fasting and prayer in the hopes of glimps-ing the heavenly light during the *Laylat ul-qadr*, the Night of Might at the end of Ramadan, the month of fasting. This was the night when the first revelation of the Quran took place, and the light of this holy night is supposed to illumi-nate the world. As it turned out, not he but his pious mother was granted the vision.

Mothers play a pivotal role in the biographies of the great Chishti saints of northern India as well. As a matter of fact, women visitors to the tomb of Qutbuddin Bakhtiyar Kaki (d. 1235) in Mehrauli near Delhi will place a bouquet of flowers on the grave of his mother and his female relatives in much the same way one honors the grave of the mother of Burhanuddin Gharib (d. 1338) in Khuldabad in the Dec-can or the tomb of Maulana Rumi's mother in Karaman (Anatolia).

Fariduddin Ganj-i Shakar, "Sugar Treasure," grew up with a pious, religiously zealous mother and thus became a great saint. He attributed his entire success to his mother, who is credited with the miraculous blinding of a thief who broke into her house. After he repented of his misdeed, she restored his sight, with the result, of course, that he con-verted to Islam. Farid's greatest disciple, Nizamuddin Auliya in Delhi (d. 1325), spent his days in the presence of his pious mother, who supported him in his spiritual exer-cises. It is said that, as soon as the new moon became visi-ble, thus inaugurating a new month, Nizamuddin used to lay his head on his mother's feet to obtain her blessings for the new month. She was, after all, "a woman who had reached God, a Rabiʿa of her day, the pride of women in the world."

Legends also tell of a miracle performed by the mother of

another northern Indian Sufi. While praying for rain during
the dry season, the Sufi in question pulled a piece of cloth
from his pocket, whereupon the rain immediately began to
fall. When asked about the secret of this cloth, he replied:
"It's my mother's skirt!" This is reminiscent of another rain
prayer attributed to the aunt of the great founder of the
Qadiriyya order, ʿAbdul Qadir Gilani (d. 1166 in Baghdad),
who, when sweeping the floor, used to exclaim: "Lord God,
I've swept it, now You sprinkle water on it!" Naturally it
immediately began to rain.

That Ibn ʿArabi's biological mother also visited and venerated his "spiritual mother," Fatima bint al-Muthanna, is a
fact documented in the biography of the great Andalusian.

Assembling an anthology of all the poems expressing the
Muslims' gratitude and love for their mothers over the cen-
turies would be a pleasant task indeed. One may think, for
example, of the verses of the tenth-century Arab poet Abu
Firas which he wrote to his beloved mother from jail, or
Iqbal's moving elegy to his mother:

> Who, waiting at home, will pray for me,
> will worry when letters tarry?
> Into your grave I'll put this question:
> Who'll remember me in her nightly prayer?

Or these unpretentious lines by the Persian poet Iraj
Mirza (d. 1926) about his mother:

> They say that, when I was born,
> my mother taught me to suck the milk.
> And every night beside my crib
> she taught me to sleep as soft as silk.
> With a smile she pressed her lips to mine
> till my mouth with joy overspilt.
> She took my hand and guided my foot
> till I learned to walk with a happy lilt.
> One word, two words, then three and more—
> that's how she taught me to talk.

> That's why my life is part of her life,
> and will remain so as long as I live.

The woman visitor never fails to be moved by the way the (sometimes illiterate) mother of a Pakistani or Turkish, an Arabian or Persian family manages the household and how respectfully her sons treat her in return, regardless of how high their social standing may be. In the purely secular world, too, in the women's quarters of the kings, it was the mother of the crown prince, be she the *Valide Sultan* of the Ottoman imperial house or the emperor's wife or the Dowager Queen of the Indian Mogul empire, who in a certain way exercised more power than the sovereign himself, and she knew how to impress the stamp of her personality on the court as well as its surroundings.

This brings us, perhaps indirectly, to the important role the wet-nurse played in Islamic history. Wet-nurses in imperial houses were frequently also distinguished patrons of the arts, and we need only think of the exquisite copy of the Quran, the so-called *mushaf al-hadina*, that the nurse of the Zirid ruler in Tunisia contracted, or of the buildings in Lahore, Mandu, and other places founded by women in Muslim India. In Mandu, in fact, there is a very beautiful architectural compound dating back to the fifteenth century known as the "Resting Place of the Wet-Nurse's Little Sister."

The Sufis not only emphasized the role of the pious mother in their literature, but they also turned to the maternal realm for some of their symbols. Didn't God say in one of the extra-Quranic revelations reported by Ghazzali: "If My servant falls sick, I care for him as a loving mother tends her son."

It was soon realized that the word *rahma*, "mercy," the root of the constantly repeated divine names *ar-rahman*, "The Compassionate," and *ar-rahim*, "The Merciful," derives from the same root as does *rahim*, "mother's womb." Rumi tells us (M IV 2923) that, just as God is always a refuge for humanity, so is the mother a refuge for her child. In fact, when this great mystical poet celebrates ecstatic death in love, he says:

> Like a child that dies on its mother's lap,
> So will I die on the lap of Mercy. (D 1639)

The death of small children was a frequent occurrence in the Middle Ages, and people tried to comfort the bereaved women with the popular belief that children who die young are lonely in Paradise and therefore draw their parents to them when they die. But the mother who dies in childbirth ranks more highly than do the virgins in Paradise, for she is counted among the martyrs, as the "Tales of the Prophets" so reassuringly report.

Mercy can be seen as a mother or a wet-nurse (M I 555) in much the same way that all-encompassing love is symbolized as the mother in Rumi's work. Love is the "primordial Mary," the mother who cares for her children—and who wouldn't like to suck at the breast of mercy, as Rumi repeatedly asks? And yet, not only abstract concepts like love and mercy are perceived as a loving mother, but the prophets as well, for they too watch over the development of the child, which is to say, over the development of the souls that have been entrusted to them. As Rumi says in his *Diwan*:

> The anger of prophets is like that of mothers,
> An anger filled with tenderness for her pretty child
>   (D 2237);

for no mother scolds her child for the fun of it, but simply to help him along. Would she let her child bloodlet if she didn't know the brief pain would do the child good (D 405)?

The prophets are not the only ones to be cast in the role of "mothers"; the master on the mystical path can also be depicted in this way. Even today, faithful Ismailis use this image when referring to the *hazir imam* Aga Khan, whom they venerate as "father and mother" and who prefaces his proclamations with "paternal and maternal blessings." Similarly, the spiritual closeness that bonds master and disciple and which introduces the disciple to the mysteries of the path can also be compared to "breast feeding" (see M I 2378). The mystical master nourishes his disciple at his breast, as Kulali said to his disciple Baha'uddin Naqsh-band (d. 1389); he offers him, as it were, the "milk of wisdom" and loving kindness.

In Rumi's *Mathnawi* (M II 2969), then, even the mother of Moses appears as the symbol of the Perfect Man, whose disciple is her own child.

According to Rumi, the human being is like a pregnant woman who carries within her the mystery that grows ever larger and ever deeper with every step. Such people are the true "men of God," those whom, as the Quran says (Sura 24:37), nothing can keep from their worship; they wear, carry, and bear the names of God in themselves, as it were.

The emotional and spiritual development of a person can also be depicted with a related image. At the beginning of the second book of Rumi's *Mathnawi*, which he continued after a four-year hiatus following the conclusion of the first book, we read: "It takes a while for blood to turn to milk" (M II 1). The pain and grief Rumi suffered in the wake of the disappearance of his friend Shamsuddin, the heart's blood he shed for his sake, had slowly turned to spiritual milk, which is to say, into something suitably wholesome and nutritious for his disciples. But not only that, for to his mind pregnancy and labor pains serve to point to the spiritual development of a person. 'Attar's already cited verse "He who is not pregnant from the pain of love, / He is a woman, he is not a man," is just another way of saying the same thing. Pain is the prerequisite for spiritual purification without which one cannot attain the rank of the true "man of God." This emphasis on pain is the focal point of many Sufi legends and tales, and all of them clearly perceive the soul as a feminine entity. After all, isn't the central experience for any woman the pain of childbirth, as Eduard Spranger suggests in his *Psychologie der Geschlechter* (Psychology of the Sexes)? This connection may sound a bit farfetched at first, but even a glance at the literature of mystical Islam shows that this whole genre, however unconsciously at times, actually did identify the human soul with the feminine element. We have seen how clearly this identification is expressed in the *nafs* theme. This, then, is the context within which Rumi's metaphor of the birth of Christ in the believer's soul is to be understood. Indeed, this Sufi mystic conceived the idea a full half century before Meister Eckhart: "The body is like Mary. Each of us has a Jesus [within], but our Jesus will not be born before we experience pain. If pain never comes, Jesus will return to his origins along the same mysterious path by which He came, and we remain behind, bereft and deprived of any benefit."

Pain is an essential aspect of all development and growth, and if Mary, having suffered the pangs of childbirth, was rewarded with a shower of sweet dates, then it follows that the sight of the beautiful Beloved will expunge all memory of pain from the soul. This is the context in which the Quranic story of the women who never even noticed they had cut their fingers when Yusuf entered their chamber is to be understood.

Further, if the soul is perceived as feminine in a metaphorical sense, then her union with God is like the conjugal union of man and woman, which in turn can lead to even greater things. To use the imagery so popular among the Sufis, "the body becomes pregnant through its connection with the spirit and brings forth good works." Every created being from minerals to man is basically a mother, for each brings forth something better from its encounter with a higher power, just as fire is engendered by the union of iron and stone. Every human act in which the active and the passive elements unite is considered a conception, and this sequence of conception and birth permeates all aspects of existence, including the union of the primordial pen with the primordial tablet. This is why even the Turkish language can call a poem that was "engendered" by a sudden act of inspiration a *doğuş*, which is to say, a "birth" or "something born," for, as Rumi knows, "whatever exists is a mother; and yet, each one is ignorant of the pains of the other" (M III 3562).

━ 7 · Woman as Manifestation of God ━━━━━━━━

THE PROPHET EXPRESSED HIS LOVE for women in very clear terms (see above, p. 10), and classical Arabic as well as early Persian literature is replete with love poems and descriptions of the sweetly perfumed beloved with all her charms. And yet a caveat is not out of place here. In the Persian and Turkish literatures it is often difficult to discern whether the venerated person is masculine or feminine, since neither the Persian nor the Turkish language has grammatical gender and only the mention of particular characteristics can clear the confusion. Such characteristics include constant allusions to the sprouting beard of the beloved (usually portrayed as an exquisitely beautiful fourteen-year-old youth). And yet, many, especially Persian, readers consider this trait little more than a useful symbol to conceal the person's true biological gender. In this regard, Hammer-Purgstall's remark in the introduction to his translation of the *Divan of Hafis* of 1812–1813 seems particularly pertinent (p. vii): "In passages that can not possibly refer to feminine beauty, [the translator] did not allow himself any alteration, which he would have had to have done if he wanted to avoid inconsistencies such as, for example, praising young girls for their budding beards."

Poets have sung ever since the eleventh century of the love the mighty Sultan Mahmud of Ghazna felt for Ayaz, his

Turkish military slave. This theme continued to appear in countless allusions, including many epic poems in Iran between the fourteenth and sixteenth centuries. And because the *nafs* can be perceived as a feminine, that is, lower, element, it is understandable to a certain degree that many verses are addressed to a male beloved.

Goethe enumerated the female versions of the ideal beloved in his *West-Östlicher Divan* by reminding his reader to:

> Listen and remember
> Six pairs of lovers . . .

namely Rustam and Rudaba (in this case, Rustam's father was Rudaba's actual husband);Yusuf and Zulaikha; Farhad and Shirin; Majnun and Laila; the Arabian poet Jamil and Buthayna; and Solomon and "the Brown One," namely, Bilqis, the queen of Southern Arabia. He then goes on to add yet a seventh couple to his list, Wamiq and ʿAzra, who are known from the Persian tradition. Of the seven couples listed above, the later literature places greatest emphasis on Majnun and Laila. The story of Qais, who is driven mad by unrequited love and becomes *majnun*, or "possessed," harks back to early Arabic traditions. He is the lover who leaves the City of Reason and takes up residence in the desert. His companions are wild beasts; birds nest in his hair; and he kisses the paws of the cur that happened to wander down Laila's street. Countless poets saw in Majnun the symbol of their own state (or so they said), and when the love-obsessed man no longer wanted so much as to see his Laila because he lived so completely in her as it was, the story came to serve the mystic as an image of his own total absorption in the Divine Beloved.

Thus Laila as well as the other women cast as the beloved in classic Arabic literature, such as Hind and Salma, turn up in Arabic mystical poetry as chiffres, or metaphors, for the Divine Being the poets so ardently yearn for. The verses of Ibn al-Farid (d. 1235) and Ibn ʿArabi are rich in allusions to Hind and Salma, to Lubna, Buthayna, and others. There are also tales about the disorienting confusion a man suffers under the shock of great love. The most familiar example of this is the story of Sheikh Sanʿan, who abandons the ascetic path because of his suddenly overwhelming love for a Christian woman. In order to win his beloved, he drinks wine at her behest and even goes so far as to herd her pigs. At the end of the story, of course, the temptress is led to the proper path and converts, and the Sheikh returns to his disciples.

This story was widely known within the eastern Islamic regions after ʿAttar gave it its classic form in his *Mantiq ut-tair*. It turns up in Kashmiri as well as Malaysian literature, and it was a moving moment when in September 1994 an Intourist guide in Bukhara related the same tale in its Chagatay-Turkish version by Mir Ali Shir Nawaʾi (d. 1501) with a great deal of personal involvement. The adventures of Sheikh Sanʿan are an impressive documentation of the overpowering force the love for a woman can exert. It must be remembered, however, that in a society where a man hardly ever got to see a well-guarded woman outside his own immediate family, the unexpected revelation of feminine beauty (and be it only in a picture!) can have a profoundly disturbing effect on the observer. My Muslim friends from conservative families tell me that this is still the case today.

The woman can also serve as a symbol of the highest goal of one's wishes and longings, and the symbolic significance of the Kaaba seems to be connected with it. One example of this can be found in Jami's version of the story of Majnun and Laila. As the lovesick Majnun during his pilgrimage approaches the black-draped Kaaba and finally stands before it, he is no longer sure whether what he sees is the Celestial Beloved or his Laila:

> O thou who sits in the bridal chamber of coquetry
> and thou who lifts the veil of mystery.
> You sat in the society of Arabs
> and thwarted the commerce of the Persians.
> Arabs and Persians turned to gaze on you
> and their longing for you bewildered their senses.

The identification of the Kaaba with the Beloved was an already familiar motif long before Jami incorporated it into his works. Medieval writers and poets have often compared the holiest shrine of Islam to a veiled bride or a desired virgin, especially when relating their experiences on the pilgrimage. This symbolic transformation often provided the additional incentive of happy anticipation in the face of a long and dangerous journey through the desert. Their goal was to touch her and to kiss her beauty mark, the black stone. Khaqani (d. 1199) was the Persian poet who most frequently employed this symbolism in his pilgrim poems. And yet doesn't popular piety also say that, at the end of time, the Kaaba will come as a bride to the Dome of the Rock in Jerusalem? This symbolism has lost none of its significance to the present day, as one recently published American anthropological study shows, and once one has become aware of the motif, countless comparisons between the pilgrimage to Mecca and a journey to the Beloved, between a veiled bride and the draped Kaaba, can be found in the poetry.

A completely different aspect of the motif of the beloved bride is the use of the expression "virgins" to denote the inner "meaning" of a book or a poem. Likening speech to the intimate bridal chamber, the Persian mystic Ahmad Ghazzali (d. 1126) was not alone in trying to entrust the undefiled virgins, which is to say, the actual meaning or sense of the work which no one prior to this particular poet had ever revealed, to the "men," which is to say, to the letters [of the alphabet]. As early as the eleventh century, the

Indo-Persian poet Abu'l-Faraj Runi (d. 1091) sought a "fresh-looking husband" for the virgin "word," and Hafiz was not the only one who tried to comb the charming locks of the "winsome bride of the word." The Urdu poet Sauda (d. 1781), on the other hand, considered his sharp tongue a scissor with which he meant to custom-cut an appropriate dress for the bride "meaning."

It was Ibn ʿArabi, however, who played the major role in explaining the significance of the feminine element with definitions that plumbed ever-deeper depths. Not only did he ascribe to the common practice of viewing the *nafs* as feminine, but he actually extended this view to encompass the *dhat*, the "divine essence," under this rubric as well. As he saw it, the feminine aspect is the form in which God can best be recognized.

This symbolism is particularly striking in the small anthology of lyric poems Ibn ʿArabi composed after his encounter with the beautiful and learned Persian woman called Nizam in Mecca. These verses sound like absolutely normal classical love poems, but Ibn ʿArabi felt compelled to add a deeper mystical-philosophical dimension to them. The reader is thus constantly confronted with images pointing to the divine-feminine: the "friendly women" he meets as he circumambulates the Kaaba are "angels who circle around the Throne" (as Sura 39:75 describes it). Even though this image turns up in some of the other works dedicated to the pilgrimage as well, it was Ibn ʿArabi who first recognized the "friendly girls" (poem XIX) as "forms of divine wisdom, which make the heart of the gnostic rejoice." "Beautiful women" can also be the "helping Names of God" (poems CLIV 2, XXVI 1), whereas the "charming women" (XXXIX 1) are meant to be understood as "divine ideas." The beloved Salma, however, is explained with a pun, as the "Solomonic site" (IV 2). And, in an ambiguous, hardly translatable exegesis, the great Andalusian says:

> My intention with this poem is to portray only her,
> (that is, the letter *ha*, the feminine pronoun),
> I have no other attachments besides the one to her,
> for my attachment to the world of phenomena
> exists entirely for her sake, because she reveals
>   herself in it. (XIII 10)

This learned statement actually expresses Ibn ʿArabi's position very well, for in another place he describes his understanding of the Divine with these words:

> God can not be seen apart from matter, and He is seen more perfectly in the human *materia* than in any other, and more perfectly in woman than in man. For He is seen either in the aspect of *agens* or in that of *patiens* or as both simultaneously. Therefore when a man contemplates God in his own person in regard to the fact that woman is produced from man, he contemplates God in the aspect of *agens*, and when he pays no regard to the production of women from himself he contemplates God in the aspect of *patiens*, because, as God's creature, he is absolutely *patiens* in relation to God, but when he contemplates God in woman, he contemplates Him both as *agens* and *patiens*. God manifested in the form of woman is *agens* in virtue of exercising complete sway over man's soul and causing man to become submissive and devoted to Himself, and He is also *patiens* because inasmuch as He appears in the form of women He is under the man's control and subject to his orders: hence to see God in woman is to see Him in both these aspects, and such vision is more perfect than seeing Him in all the forms in which He manifests Himself. (MC 1:155-56)[1]

Similar thoughts are echoed here and there in Rumi's work as well. One example is the tale (M I 2436) in which the poet, though somewhat critical of women in his exege-

---

[1] Quoted in Annemarie Schimmel, *Mystical Dimensions of Islam* (Chapel Hill, N.C., 1975), p. 431.

sis of a saying of the Prophet, suddenly conjures up a completely different image and sings:

> She is a ray of God, she is not that (earthly) beloved:
> She is creative, you might say she is not created.

Passages previous to this had mentioned the Prophet's
ecstatic experience, whereupon the poet observed: "On the
night of the *ta'ris* his holy spirit gained (the privilege of)
kissing hands in the presence of the Bride" (M I 1991). Yet,
he adds cautiously: "If I have called Him (God) the Bride, do
not find fault."[2]

The same idea is also evident in Rumi's treatment of the
mystical state, *hal*, and of the lasting stage, *maqam*, "sta-
tion," on the mystical path when he says: "The *hal* is like
the unveiling of the beauteous bride, / while the *maqam* is
the (king's) being alone with the bride" (M 1 1435).[3] In other
words, during *hal* the mystic is briefly conscious of the
beauty of the Divine Beloved, but in *maqam* he can hope for
enduring revelations, for mystical union (M 1 1435).

Such thoughts are strewn throughout Rumi's work and,
as so often with him, are rather unsystematically touched
on here and there, whereas Ibn 'Arabi finds this interplay
between the masculine and the feminine everywhere. The
reader is thus reminded of ancient myths of the androgy-
nous creator-god. One is tempted to say that the *yang* and
yin principle is evident in all things. Not only Ibn 'Arabi but
countless other Muslims have recognized this duality, which
appears when the Absolute Oneness of the *deus absconditus* reveals itself in the forms of *jamal*, divine beauty, and
jalal, divine majesty, or else as *lutf*, divine kindness, and
qahr, divine wrath—terms that anticipate Rudolf Otto's dif-

---

[2] Quoted in *The Mathnawi of Jalaluddin Rumi*, edited from the Oldest
Manuscripts, with Critical Notes, Translation and Commentary by
Reynold A. Nicholson (London, 1925; reprint, E. J. W. Gibb Memorial
Series, New Series [n.p.], 1968), pp. 133, 108.

[3] Quoted in Schimmel, *Mystical Dimensions*, p. 79.

ferentiation of the *mysterium tremendum* and the *mysterium fascinans*. And doesn't the creative word *kun*, "be!," which in Arabic consists of two letters, *kn*, also point to the twofold manifestation of the One? Heartbeat and breath, sun and rain, health and sickness all point to this mystery, without which life as we know it would be unimaginable. Day and night are equally dependent upon one another. Thus, when the Persian-Turkish proverb says, "The nights are pregnant," we are involuntarily reminded of the myth of the emergence of creation from all-encompassing night.

Ibn ʿArabi interpreted the Prophet's words referring to his love for women on the basis of his own conception of the central role of the feminine components of the Divine, and he expressed his thoughts about sexual love in explicit terms as well. Later mystical writers expanded on these ideas, frequently embellishing them with graphic descriptions, and have alluded to the mysteries of the physical relation between husband and wife. A typical example of this can be seen in the short work by the Kashmir Sufi Yaʿqub Sarfi (d. 1594) that Sachiko Murata analyzed in her study. Yaʿqub Sarfi uses the "religious" experience of physical love to explain the need for a complete bath after intercourse: during this ecstatic event, which is the highest joy available and attainable to the human being, the spirit is so completely involved with the manifestations of the Divine that it loses all connection to its physical embodiment. The only way to return this corpselike body to normal life is to perform complete ablutions. Sarfi naturally knows that this kind of spiritualized physical union is reserved only for the chosen few; mere mortals are not privy to the experience. Other mystics of the Ibn ʿArabi school would probably agree with him in this. Sarfi's depiction almost reminds the reader of tantric rites, and several ideas prevalent in Kashmirian Tantrism or Shivaism may even have crept into his work. Similar ideas about the "mystery of marriage" can be found in the work of Kasani (d. 1543), a mystic who hailed from Farghana. After all, wasn't Eve created so that "Adam might find comfort in her," as the Quran says (Sura 7:189)? She was the divine gift sent to comfort him in his loneliness; she was the manifestation of that divine ocean which he had left—and hence her greatness. The Divine, as Ibn ʿArabi was well aware, reveals itself most beautifully in woman.

∼ 8 · The Brides of God ∼⎯⎯⎯⎯⎯⎯

I N IBN ʿARABIʾS CONCEPTUAL WORLD, the woman becomes the highest, sublime *object* of masculine yearning; she becomes the personification of the Divine, which encompasses within Itself active and passive, masculine and feminine traits. But can't such a "sophianic" attitude toward the feminine lead to the subjugation of women in the hands and minds of less high-minded men if the spiritual component is no longer, or not yet, recognized?

There is yet another way to restore to the "woman" her intrinsic value, another way to shape her into the idealized "man of God." After all, isn't the soul, like its earthly counterpart, the woman, also a seeking, yearning *subject*, constantly looking for the path that leads to the Divine Beloved, even though this path might involve trials and tribulations?

"Longing is the feminine side of love, the cup that waits to be filled" writes Llewellyn Vaughan-Lee, thus touching on what I think is a central theme within the complex of "women and Sufism." In fact, in this context it would be wrong to speak only of the factual role women play in Islamic mysticism, just as it would be simply to list the names of the great women mystics whose deeds and existence have been mentioned over the centuries throughout the Islamic world, or to restrict our thoughts solely to the

respect shown to the mother or the old woman, which is
another, constantly reiterated theme in Islamic literature.
And hasn't it been said that "only women can truly experience love, that pure form of devotion that makes her burn
with desire while denying all hope of fulfillment?" This is
the question Ed. Dimock raises in his study of the mysticism of the (admittedly Hindu) Bengalis.

The idea that Eve, created from Adam's rib and thus a
part of him, constantly yearns for the undivided whole is an
old one indeed. Perhaps this longing of the part for the
whole is greater than that of the whole for the part that was
taken away. This is reminiscent of gnostic ideas about the
splitting of the primal principle into the two aspects of the
heavenly masculine and the earthly feminine. The feminine
soul is lost in the darkness of the world, enticeable, prone
to the lower instincts, as the Nag Hammadi texts insinuate,
and yet she still yearns for her actual Lord, with whom she
can once again experience the previously lost and squandered bliss of union. The tenets of gnosticism have good
reason to speak of the mysterious sacrament of the bridal
chamber, and centuries later Rumi took up the same theme
when he wrote that no one except the eunuch "Grief"
(D 1405) may enter the bed chamber when the soul engages
in her loving gambles with the Divine Spirit (D 195) and
where she and her Beloved come together in conjugal
union.

How could "Lady Soul," who resides in the palace of the
body, stay there when her Beloved calls?

> Lady Soul, who sat in the palace of the body,
> took off her veil and ran away for love. (D 1198)

Rumi also reincarnated the mythical *hieros gamos* in his
poetry:

> You are the sky, I am the amazed earth,
> What makes you grow ever fresh in my heart?

> How should the earth know what you have sewn
>   in her heart?
> It's enough that you know it. You have impregnated
>   her! (D 3048)

For, as he says many years later in another verse:

> The sky is masculine and the earth a woman;
> Whatever he casts into it brings forth fruit.

In his *Mathnawi* (M III 4401-4404) Rumi tells how every created thing desires its mate, just like iron and the magnet, like amber and straw, like heaven and earth; and only such a union can result in offspring of a higher order. Although Rumi symbolizes the soul's union with God through the image of human intercourse, his attention remains focused on the feminine aspect of the soul and not so much, as with Ibn ʿArabi, on the role of woman as an idealized object of love. Rumi's father, Baha-i Walad, whose thoughts and feelings most profoundly influenced the great mystic, writes: "As the bride sees all the hidden parts of her husband and the husband all the hidden parts and pudenda of his bride and both are unafraid and free and joyful in their mutual play—so too when He sees all your hidden and private parts, prostrate yourself before God, without shame or bashfulness." Isn't there an echo of this in his son's verses:

> With you I prefer to be naked;
> I toss off the garb from my frame
> so that the lap of Your grace
> turns into a garment for my soul? (D 551)

These images must have been very widespread among the Sufis, for five centuries after Rumi Muhammad Nasir ʿAndalib in Delhi (d. 1758) wrote in his novel *Nala-yi ʿAndalib* (The Lamentation of the Nightingale) that, in the moment of consummation, the bride recognizes her husband as the mighty Lord and understands his terrible majesty, whereas beforehand she only knew his kindness. He, then, explains to her that his seeming cruelty in piercing her body is nothing other than a sign of overpowering love which reveals itself in the "naked [act] of union."

In a certain sense, ʿAndalib's words recall Bernini's statue of Saint Teresa, who, though pierced by an arrow, bears the expression of sublime bliss. (The arrow motif is associated with love in just about every culture, be it Amor in the classical Greek and Roman tradition or Kama in the Hindu; after all, the final experience, physical as well as emotional, is always one of "blissful pain.") The Indian subcontinent is particularly renowned for the genuine bridal mysticism that emerged there. In it the soul, bound to the Divine Beloved ever since the primordial covenant (Sura 7:172), waits for the wedding, which popular tales describe in full worldly detail: cloths are spread about, delicious foods prepared, rose water is sprinkled everywhere.

The union of the soul with God is not the only phenomenon represented through the image of physical consummation, for among the Persian Sufis the intimate relation between a master and his disciple is also called a "spiritual marriage," *izdiwaj ruhani.*

Weren't the friends of God also called "the brides of God," who could be seen by none other than their closest relatives? This is the way the great north Iranian mystic Bayezid Bistami (d. 874) put it. To be sure, in Ibn ʿArabi's system these "brides" constitute a very specific category of saints, the *afrad*, or "single ones," whom God has concealed under the veil of censure so that they can in no way be differentiated from normal people. In fact, they can even take on the form of seeming enemies.

And yet it is precisely the idea of the bride soul, whose one and only Beloved is God Himself, that has led to the custom of designating death as ʿurs, "wedding"—a spiritual wedding in which the soul is finally reunited with her primordial Beloved. Rumi sings:

> Don't say "Farewell" when I am put in the grave,
> A curtain is it for eternal bliss.

Everything that is separate from God, that has been cast out of the primal union and into a world of time and space by the very act of creation, yearns for the lost whole. In the Ismaili poetry of Indo-Pakistan, the *virahini*, the woman yearning in unfulfilled love, can be understood as a symbol of creation separated from God.

In order to understand fully this idea of feminine yearning and receptivity, we might want to reconsider more closely the symbols as well as the way the poets and mystics used them to suggest a person's relation to his or her beloved:

> When you see your Beloved,
> Sit before him like a mirror!

This is the way Rumi put it. The mirror, though, has always had an important function in the history of religions. In Japan, for example, the mirror is the attribute of the Sun Goddess Amaterasu and is thus connected with a female deity. Thus it has come to be a typically feminine utensil, for its single task is to reflect the image of the beloved without adding anything of its own to that reflection. In ancient Egypt mirrors were always among the accouterments placed in the tomb along with the body, for they were supposed to capture and preserve the rays of the sun as it traveled its path through the underworld. This idea is not foreign to the Western world, either, for in some churches (such as Aix-la-Chapelle during a specific pilgrimage) people used to "catch" and "carry" relics in small mirrors. Similarly, then, the human heart, defiled by worldly thoughts and deeds, has to be polished of its rust, of the verdigris of secular relations, by constantly thinking of God. (Medieval mirrors, we recall, were made of metal.) This polishing was meant to prepare them (the mirrors [or the hearts]) to take in the Light of God. When the poets, and here again most frequently Rumi, tell the story of how a guest could bring no better gift than a mirror to the beautiful Yusuf, himself the manifestation of Divine Beauty, so that he might admire his own good looks, the role of the yearning, receptive heart could not be more clearly depicted.

The idea of the world's reflecting the downward stream of divine light so that it might return again into the heights is only one aspect of Neoplatonic thought, and it explains why the Sufis, especially those who followed Ibn ʿArabi's ideas, compare this created world to a mirror. For them, the relative nonexistence, in other words the feminine element, becomes a mirror capable of reflecting the divine names that emanated from the *deus absconditus* during the moment of creation. It is only through the light of these names that relative nonexistence acquires contingent existence; it would disappear if the radiance of the names were taken from it, which is just another way of saying, if the mirror were to try to postulate an existence of its own in the absence of the Divine Manifestation. Only via that side of creation that is turned toward God can one glean some idea of the glory of the Creator "as through a mirror"—at least for those "who have eyes to see."

Medieval Sufis expanded this image. The reverse sides of ancient metallic mirrors were often richly decorated, frequently with astronomical, hunting, or other secular motifs. Poets took advantage of this fact to compare people solely concerned with worldly matters to fools who take pleasure in the ornamented side of the mirror without recognizing or even having any idea of its reverse side, its true meaning, which is, of course, the reflection of Divine Beauty. Maulana Rumi takes up the famous extra-Quranic word of God that Ibn ʿArabi had used as the focal point of his creation myth by having God say to David: "I was a hidden treasure and wanted to be seen, therefore I created the world!" This is the way Rumi put it in one of his quatrains:

> I created a mirror, clear to you;
> its face is the heart, its back the world,
> yet, unless you know the face, my Friend,
> you prefer the back!

This is why the ideal lover turns his heart into an unblemished polished mirror in which he finds reflected the beloved, who is now closer to him than he is to himself. One of the Persian quatrains of Mir Dard claims:

> I spent a lifetime listening to Him from afar,
> Only in my dreams I drew Him close to my breast.
> Now, since only I stood as mirror before Him
> He saw Himself, but I did not see Him.

Isn't the lover's heart also like the pure water, another feminine element, that acts as a mirror? The mystics of all religions had good reason to invoke the metaphor of the moon, whose reflection is mirrored in every body of water, be it the wide ocean or a small puddle. Its reflection can also appear in every soul, be it in ever so weak or distorted an image. Rumi says:

> My heart is like water, clear and limpid,
> like the water that reflects the moon.

Ahmad Ghazzali (d. 1126) alluded to the mystery of reflection in his *Sawanih*, "Aphorisms on Love," and in the entire corpus of mystical poetry the mirror, that womanly utensil, is the preferred image for the union of the lover with the beloved. Put another way, in many instances the lover is subconsciously, perhaps even totally unconsciously, perceived as feminine, as the receptive, yearning bride-soul.

The mirror, however, is not the only symbol of receptive woman-souls. Other images come into play here, too,

including that of musical instruments, most markedly perhaps in Rumi's musically oriented compositions. It is no
accident that the *Mathnawi* begins with the "Song of the
Reed-flute," for the flute, once used in the Phrygian cult
during the epiclesis of the divinity, is an exquisite symbol of
the soul cut off from its primordial roots and constantly
singing of its yearning for its lost homeland:

> I seek a heart, torn asunder by severance,
> that I may tell it of the agony of my yearning.

Rumi knew himself to be like the flute that could produce
music only when touched by the breath of the beloved.
Only when "that one, that Turk" inspires him, can he
speak, can he sing of his longing for his homeland. Other
instruments become equally eloquent only when stroked by
the hand of the beloved. Even if their use as symbols is not
as striking and as organic as is that of the flute and the
reed bed from which it was cut, the images of the harp, the
lute, and the rebeck can still serve the same purpose as
embodiments of the yearning soul. Could they make music
if the beloved didn't touch, stroke, or beat them? And Rumi
begs his beloved not to treat him, the little drum, too
roughly, not to abuse him with fists. One can say that this
whole group of images, "man as instrument" (sometimes
carried so far as to liken the nerves or the veins to strings),
is also part of the feminine sphere.

Mysticism has yet another favorite image, that of the
flame and the moth. This metaphor is familiar to Western
romantic poetry, but it can actually be traced back to a
chapter in the *Kitab at-tawasin* by the martyred mystic al-
Hallaj, who was executed in 922. Classical antiquity had
already used the moth metaphor to symbolize the soul, the
psyche, that floats off in death. In Hallaj's metaphor, on the
other hand, the moth comes so close to the flame of Divine
Beauty that it actually merges with the fire, thus experienc-
ing total "de-becoming."

Surely all of these images and symbols hark back to ancient mythic ideas, but the proper reading of them helps us understand better the deeper meaning many of the mystics sought to convey through their words. Whether consciously aware of it or not, the lovesick mystic is a "feminine" figure, and this is nowhere so clearly demonstrated as in the case of Rumi, regardless of how strange or absurd such an assertion may sound. In his theological and theoretical verses he naturally often employs Ibn ʿArabi's technical terminology, which was gaining in popularity and significance at that time, but in his own life Rumi experienced the mystery of reception, of inspiration as no other before him. The *hieros gamos* occurs between the Beloved, seen as the sky, and himself, who is like the earth waiting to be impregnated, and the theme of the polished mirror as a gift for Yusuf turns up in his works no fewer than three times. In fact, Rumi applies the Yusuf-Zulaikha motif to himself and his love. Toward the beginning of his *Mathnawi* Rumi's disciple Husamuddin—"the one who had caught the perfume of Yusuf's shirt" (which is to say, the one who had learned about Rumi's first beloved, Shamsuddin)—asks him about this very "Yusuf," but Maulana warns his beloved disciple not to delve any more deeply into this aspect of his life, for

> It's better that the friend remain in veils!
> You listen to the content of the tales:
> It's better that his mysteries be told
> In other people's stories, tales of old!

In all of the more than twenty-five thousand verses of this great didactic poem, Shamsuddin's name is never even mentioned. Shortly before the end of the *Mathnawi*, though—and that means shortly before the end of Maulana's life—the poet once again returns to the story of Yusuf and Zulaikha, after both his early lyrics as well as the *Mathnawi* contained countless references to the Friend whose

"beauty transcended that of Yusuf many times over."
Toward the end of the last book of this enormous work,
Rumi turns to Zulaikha and describes her life with unfor-
gettable tenderness; whatever she says or does has a direct
reference to Yusuf:

> . . . And when she said: "The wax is melting softly!"
> That was to say: "My friend was kind to me,"
> And when she said: "Look, how the moon is rising!"
> And when she said: "The willow is now green!"
> And when she said: "The leaves are a-trembling!"
> And when she said: "How lovely burns the rue . . ."
> And when she said: "The birds sang for the roses."
> And when she said: "Beat firmly all my rugs!"
> And when she said: "The bread is all unsalted."
> And when she said: "The spheres are going wrong . . ."
> She praised something—that meant: His sweet
>   embracing:
> She blamed something—that meant: He's far away.
> . . . . . .
> And when she heaped a hundred thousand names,
> Her whole intention was but Yusuf's name.
> When hungry, she but mentioned Yusuf's name,
> She would be filled, and drunken from his cup.
> In winter time his name became her fur coat.
> That's what his name does when you are in love!

And yet all of this is but the resolution of the verse that
was written seventeen years before:

> It's better that the mysteries be told
> In other people's stories, tales of old.

Whatever he said and related in the thousands of preced-
ing lines is nothing more than the paraphrase of his feelings for his first true Beloved, for Shams, whom he
considered the manifestation of the glory of God. This holds
true regardless of how strong an influence Husamuddin
may have exerted on the secular plan as *zia*, "a ray of the

for all wistfully pining woman-souls in Persian and Turkish literature, but this theme has become truly central to the mystical poetry of the Indian subcontinent. We can assume that the Indian representations of Krishna and his playful dance with the gopis (i.e., cowgirls) played a part in this development, for in every instance the gopis perceive their ever-elusive and ever-fascinating god in the very shape or form they yearn for at the moment. And Radha, the soul of his choice, finally enjoys the longed-for union with her beloved after a long time of ardent desire and solitude. This tradition is enriched by the motif of the bride-soul, the *virahini*, a theme already familiar from the folkloric literature of India. In fact, the frequently illustrated *barahmasa* poems describe the feelings of a young woman or bride who yearns for her husband or her beloved. This imagery contributed to an especially fascinating development in the Sufi poetry of the subcontinent because it was so eminently identifiable with the traditional role of the woman as a *nafs* symbol.

The mystical poets of the Indus Valley and the Punjab as well as the Sufis who had settled in the Deccan, the southern region of the Indian subcontinent, as early as the fourteenth century all took up the motif of the woman-soul, but each in their own way. In the Deccan the focus lay primarily in the region surrounding Bijapur, the capital city of the Adil Shah dynasty ever since 1490. It was here that the earliest masters of the two leading Sufi orders, the Indian Chishtis and the Qadiris, settled. The literature that originated there in the fifteenth century addressed God as "Master" and "Father" as well as "Lover," *muhibb*, and "Beloved," *mahbub*, and the works that Miranji Shams ul-'Ushshaq, "Sun of Lovers," composed in the Dakhni Urdu vernacular in the fifteenth century take up the theme of woman-souls. His *Khush* and *Khushnaghz* tell of a pious young maiden who abandons the world in order to devote herself to the spiritual life. Miranji's descendant, Burhanuddin Janam (d. 1579), was the first to present the theme of the bride-soul in a more detailed treatment in his epic poem *Sukh sahela.* Similar verses have been attributed to Gesudaraz of Gulbarga, the great saint of the Deccan who died a centenarian in 1422, but this attribution does not bear up under scholarly scrutiny.

Even so, a lyrical tradition developed alongside works that did satisfy these loftier, higher literary claims. This lyric tradition sought to transmit mystical teachings—especially those of love mysticism—to the common folk. Village women who could identify with the hard-working, long-suffering, and yearning soul were surely attracted to these verses, which they, in turn, could sing during their work.

Songs of this type fall mainly into two groups: the *chakki-nama* and the *charkhinama.* The *chakki* is the millstone women had to use every day to grind grain for the preparation of the flat *chapathis,* their main source of nutrition. The perpendicular handle of the millstone could be compared to the *alif,* the first letter of the Arabic alphabet, which is simply a perpendicular stroke. But since it is the first letter of the alphabet and thus has the numerical value of 1, the *alif* is also the symbol for the One and Unique God. The woman—so the poets' intention—should grasp this handle and concentrate all her thoughts on God while grinding her grain. The axle around which the stone revolves corresponds to the Prophet Muhammad, who received the divine message and then passed it on.

The degree to which these simple metaphors could be elaborated was completely dependent upon the talent of the individual poet. The act of grinding grain was not the only one that received symbolic significance, however, for now and again baking was also included in the imagery.

The woman of the house was supposed to act as if she were preparing *puri,* little filled pockets of dough fashioned from the freshly milled grain:

The *chakki*'s handle resembles *alif*, which means Allah;
And the axle is Muhammad, and is fixed there.
In this way the truth-seeker sees the relationship.
     Ya *bism Allah*, hu hu Allah.
We put the grains in the *chakki*,
To which our hands are witnesses.
The *chakki* of the body is in order
When you follow the *shariʿat*.
     Ya *bism Allah*, hu hu Allah.
The name of Allah comes from *alif*.
Know that *pirs* and *murshids* can lead our lives.
Grind the flour and then sift it—
     Ya *bism Allah*, hu hu Allah.

. . . . . .

Grind the flour and make stuffed *puri;*
Put in it heavenly fruits and sugar,
The seven qualities of God must be taken in the body
     As the seven ingredients fill the *puri*, Oh sister.
     Ya *bism Allah*, hu hu Allah.[1]

The image of spinning could also enter into the daily life of
women as seamlessly as did that of grinding grain. In every
culture, spinning seems to be one of the woman's social
activities, for it allows her to sing or chat with her companions while doing her work. And even though mystical spinning-wheel poems were known in southern India, they were
much more important in Sind and in the Punjab—areas
where cotton had been cultivated since time immemorial.
Nor should we forget that the spinning and combing of cotton also reminded the mystics, at least subconsciously, of
the great mystic Hallaj, who had to pay for his overwhelming
love (and his political activities) with his life in 922. His
name means "cotton-carder," and the Sufis sometimes
spoke of Hallaj's thread. This reference probably con-

---

[1] Quoted from Richard Maxwell Eaton, *Sufis of Bijapur 1300–1700:
Social Roles of Sufis in Medieval India* (Princeton, 1978), p. 163.

tributed a certain share to the popularity of the spinning-wheel poems. The Panjabi Sufi Bullhe Shah points out that the freshly picked cotton is white, and only during the spinning, dyeing, and weaving of it do its structure and color change. Bullhe Shah likens this process to the emerging of creation from God, who, "mono-toned," lies at the base of everything. Other Sufis, including the Sindhi-Naqshbandi Master Muhammad Zaman Lunwari, liked to look upon the world as the yarn that was spun from the cotton "God."

Even more important is the association of spinning with *dhikr*, the continuous remembrance of God, for the Quran enjoins the believers to "remember God often" (Sura 33:41, among others). The soft repetition of the names of God or of a religious mantra could be likened to the humming of the spinning wheel, and just as the thread is made ever finer through constant spinning, so is the heart of man made ever purer through constant recollection of God, until God "buys" it "at a good price." This last expression is a reference to Sura 9:112, according to which God "buys" the human soul. The lazy girl, though, the one who lets external temptations distract her from her spinning, will have no dowry on her wedding day (which is to say, the day she dies). She will stand naked and disgraced before God and will be rejected. (By the way, the Panjabi poet Madho Lal Husain also speaks of "coloring" the dowry textiles, and whoever fails to do so will remain unmarried.)

The idea of "the weaving of deeds" is well known in the history of religions and is surely at work here too. According to it, every person weaves out of one's thoughts, words, and deeds a garment for one's soul. One spinning poem from Bijapur elaborates upon these metaphors rather precisely:

> Imagine that your body is a spinning wheel, Oh sister.
> We should get rid of our negligence
> And give up worldly differences, Oh sister.

...

> The breath is the unspun thread for the message
> of God;
> The tongue is the rim of the spinning wheel.
> Bring out the thread of breath and show it, Oh sister.[2]

The poet then instructs the souls about all aspects of weaving:

> As you take the cotton, you should do *dhikr-i jali!*
> (that is, proclaim God in a loud voice)
> As you separate the cotton, you should do *dhikr-i qalbi!*
> (that is, repeat the Name of God in your heart)
> As you spool the threat you should do *dhikr-i 'aini!*
> (that is, your whole being should be submerged
> in the remembrance of God)
> The threads of breath should be counted one by one,
> Sister![3]

(—because inherent in every breath should be the Name of God. The rules for remembering God by means of breath control have been worked out in precise detail.)

Spinning-wheel songs in Sindhi and Panjabi are less learned. The comprehensive *Sur Kapaiti* of Shah 'Abdul Latif would require a long analysis, and many spinning songs of the Panjabi Sufis are full of ecstatic exclamations.

> Stop your playing, spin the wheel, girl!
> Hurry and finish your bridal gown, girl!
> The turning spindle hums: "O Lord!"
> trembling in fear of the Lord, O girl!
> And the draft of the spindle is like a sigh—
> You've got a lot of hard work ahead, girl!

---

[2] Ibid.

[3] Quoted from Annemarie Schimmel, *As Through a Veil: Mystical Poetry in Islam* (New York, 1982), p. 145

And yet, whether in spinning or in grinding grain, all vernacular poems portray the woman as servant:

> You are the servant in your dervish's house—
> Say Allah and the name of the Prophet
> with every breath!

In many instances, to see the woman as a "servant" is not
only sociologically correct but theologically appropriate as
well, for the Quran repeatedly designates man in general as
ʿabd, "servant, slave," with the word *amat* being the feminine equivalent. ʿ*Ubudiyya*, absolute "servantship," is the
true essence of freedom, claims the Persian mystic
Qushayri (d. 1074); and if servantship is the essential qual-
ity of a person, then to become ʿ*abduhu*, "His [God's] slave,"
is the highest stage to which a human being can aspire.
This was the name the Prophet was called during his two
most sublime experiences: once during the nocturnal flight
to heaven (Sura 17:1), which led him into the immediate
presence of God, and once during the great revelation mentioned in Sura 53. This is why the word "servant girl or
woman" is often considered the noblest designation for a
loving soul:

> Sometimes He bars the gates,
> Sometimes He opens them for me.
> Sometimes I come in vain,
> But then He calls me to the highest place.
> Sometimes I long for His summons,
> Sometimes He tells me secret words—
> See—that's how He is,
> My Friend!
>
> Beloved, you are a king's son,
> And I wear the clothes of a slave.
> I will obey your every command
> And stand ready with folded arms.
> Would I ever leave your door,

> O Friend, for even a moment?
> O Beloved, never withdraw
> Your loving glance from me.

With these words Shah ʿAbdul Latif praises the very essence of God, in whose presence the soul can do nothing other than wait silently until He should reveal Himself. In all the poems stemming from the lowlands of Pakistan, the beloved appears as "Lord"; he is "Baluchi," "Rajput," or simply "King." On the other hand, the loving woman always belongs to a lower caste and is either a washerwoman, the daughter of a potter, or even a Mohana woman, a member of the fishing folk on the Indus.

The beloved is indescribably proud and beautiful, and the loving woman sings:

> If you were to come, Beloved, with me on your mind,
> I would lay my eyelashes at your feet,
> And spread my hair upon the ground.

The image of the loving soul pervades the whole corpus of vernacular Sufi poetry. It appears also in the *ginans*, the religious songs of the Ismaili (Agakhani) community in the western part of the subcontinent. Thus, in the *Bujh Niranjan*, the soul sings:

> Lord, I have neither beauty nor virtue!
> How could I say: "Beloved, come into my house?"
> If I were to reach you through your kindness
> I would celebrate by singing wedding songs.

How could the poor soul hope to unite with the eternally beloved? She invokes Him again and again by His name *sattar*, "He who covers," one of the divine names frequently used with specific reference to women.

> Turn and enter, O husband,
> The room in this hut of mine, O wretched me.
> Beloved! Cover me, darling,
> With your hem!

Doesn't He cover all the faults of the sinful woman?

The soul is even called a sweeper, which is the word used to denote the untouchable, casteless servant who cleans the house and the latrines. The Panjabi Bullhe Shah (who sometimes dressed up in women's clothing) does not hesitate to describe himself as such a miserable woman-soul. And yet this same poet is fond of alluding to the old tale about the luckless pair of lovers, Hir and Ranjha, and dares invite the Beloved to enter her house, to attach the hem of his garments to that of hers and thus to marry her:

> If I am your beloved—
>   Come into my courtyard!
> I sacrifice myself to you—
>   Come into my courtyard!
>
> There is no other like You!
> I've looked for You in the jungle,
> I've looked for you everywhere—
> Come into my courtyard!
>   I sacrifice myself to you—
>   Come into my courtyard!
>
> They call You Cow-herd—
> But I say Ranjha,
> For you are my faith—
> Come into my courtyard.
>   I sacrifice myself to you—
>   Come into my courtyard!
>
> I left my parents,
> And attached my hem to yours.
> Have mercy on my longing—
> Come into my courtyard!
>   I sacrifice myself to you—
>   Come into my courtyard!

The image of critical or scolding parents or neighbors is another popular motif that entered the Persian literature via a more realistic interpretation of the "reprimander" so familiar to Arabic poetry. But what is the loving girl supposed to do? The Panjabi Sufi Ali Haidar (d. 1781) embroiders his song with the theme of Hir and Ranjha as well:

> People are already tired of warning me—
> Yet I continue to contemplate
> my beautiful Friend!
> And if my parents throw me out of the house,
> I'll gladly leave their abode
> for my darling Friend.
>
> I'll toss those who scold me into the well!
> I want to stay in the wilderness
> with my Friend.
> Ali Haidar, since the day our eyes met
> I will never break my promise,
> O Friend!

References to the refractory attitude of the girl who flees from the world to be with her beloved can be found in the *ginans* as well. In Gujerat the girl could leave home with a water jug on her head and could go to her beloved, who was then obliged to take her in.

This image leads fairly directly into the symbolism that is used in the marriage poems or songs. A comparison of the expressions used in the actual Sindhi wedding songs with those in the mystical literature reveals many similarities. This is particularly true in the case of Khwaja Ghulam Farid (d. 1901), a popular folk poet who wrote his simple verses in Siraiki, an expressive dialect located between Sindhi and Panjabi. Farid's woman-soul asks for colorful shawls from Ajmer and bangles from Jaisalmer, for his native Cholistan borders on present-day Rajasthan in India. His heroines speak of the nose ring the abandoned married woman no longer wants to wear; they speak of dyeing their hair, of lip rouge, and of the black antimony used to darken their eyelashes. These are the true women of the Cholistan desert, one of whom says in reference to a marriage rite:

> We used to bump heads
> back in preeternity!

(An important part of the marriage ceremony has the bride and groom bump their heads together.)

All girl-souls use a typically girlish vernacular. They continuously address their sisters (*bhenar*), playmates (*satiyun*), and girlfriends (*adiyan*), and occasionally scold them for failing to understand what it's like to be a true lover. Listen to the soul in *Bujh Niranjan*:

> *dekʰha sakʰhi suheliyan dʰhan ko hal behal*
> Behold, happy companions, the wretched state
> of [this] woman!

In such instances girlfriends symbolize those who are satisfied with their everyday life, the ones who cannot comprehend how a heroic soul would want to leave her normal life behind and embark "manfully" on the difficult path leading to the Divine Beloved simply because she is unable to resist the attractive force of God's love, whereas the material world strikes her as being of no consequence. This is exactly the way Rumi described Bilqis's motives for undertaking her journey (see p. 44). Thus, the affectionate but ignorant sisters and playmates serve a real purpose in many mystical poems and songs. Shah ʿAbdul Karim (d. 1694) also adds a warning note to the verses his Sindhi woman-soul sings:

> His footprints are everywhere, sisters,
> But they're difficult to discover.
> Even after seeing them with your own eyes
> You still don't understand their significance.

Like real women, woman-souls are fond of diminutives, those commonly used linguistic expressions of tenderness that can even be found in the Arabic mystical love poems of Ibn al-Farid. Punhun, the prince of Kecch in Balochstan, is affectionately referred to as *Punhal* or *Balochal*, "dear little

Baluch," or even *Khohyariyal,* "dear mountaineer," and nicknames are forever being invented for the beloved hero. Many of these women, especially those in Sindhi poetry, are prone to using the endearing diminutive suffix *rro, rri,* and not only when talking about their beloved. They frequently change the name of the crow (*kang*), the traditional messenger bird, to *kangal* or *kangrri.*

In Urdu poetry the use of *rekhti,* the woman's dialect, is generally limited to frivolous themes and topics, but Urdu mystical folk poetry incorporates it as an integral part of the atmosphere. The soul, dazed by the beauty of her beloved, sings:

> When my coy Beloved
>   sets out on his way,
> The ground murmurs "in the name of God"
>   and the path kisses his foot.
> With most delicate decorum
>   the confused and confounded huris
>   rise as he passes.
>   I swear by the Almighty: my Beloved
> Is truly the most beautiful of all.

The poets of the Indo-Pakistani subcontinent have many different ways of expressing their feelings, but all of them follow Indian patterns and use Indian meters. On the other hand, unknown in the popular folk tradition is the *ghazal,* that is, the classical type of lyric poem with complicated meters and mono-rhyme. This form was appropriated from Arabic-Persian literature and has been popular among circles of educated urbane poets for centuries.

In addition to the short two-line *dohas,* we also have longer stanzaic poems like the *siharfi* and the *barahmasa.* The *siharfi,* the "Thirty Letter Poem," is a type of Golden Alphabet in which each stanza ideally begins with a different letter of the Arabic alphabet. As often happens, though, several stanzas will begin with the same letter, and the length of the stanza itself depends completely on the personal preference of the poet. The theme of the loving soul is common in these poems too, but it forms a more integral component of the *barahmasa*, the "Twelve Month Poem." This form was taken over from Sanskrit and became widespread in most Indian languages. Its sole theme is the expression of the various emotional states of the *virahini*, the unsatisfied, longing woman. Each month brings its own peculiar trials, and love, yearning, and sadness are celebrated in keeping with the character and the nature of the month in question. This was an appropriate way to express human emotions as long as the poet followed the natural sequence of the year and took advantage of the fact that in the Indian tradition the rainy period is most closely associated with yearning and with union with one's beloved. People believe the Papiha bird sings *piu kahan*, "Where is my Beloved?" during the rainy season. Thus, when the great Indo-Persian poet Amir Khosrau (d. 1325) begins his collection of poems with the line: "It's raining, and I am separated from my Friend . . . ," he is weaving the *virahini* motif into his highly complicated Persian poetry.

Symbolism becomes more abstruse when poets adopt the Islamic lunar calendar, for its monthly divisions are independent of the seasons and, being purely lunar months, they annually fall out of step with the solar year by ten or eleven days. To overcome this difficulty, poets simply transformed the ancient nature symbolism into concrete historical allusions. In Muharram, for instance, the bride-soul grieves for the martyrdom of Husain, the Prophet's grandson, who was killed on the tenth day of Muharram 81 (October 10, 680) by government troops in Kerbela. In the third lunar month, one either contemplates death or, in a more sanguine mood, the birth of the Prophet, who often appears in later popular poetry as the beloved, the actual longed-for groom of the bride-soul: *dulah nabi rasul*, "bridegroom, messenger, prophet" as he is also called in the *Bujh Niranjan*. The highest goal the later Sufis could hope to attain was "de-becoming in the Prophet" and no longer, as in classical times, "de-becoming in God." Ramadan, the holy month of fasting, is the cause of high praise, and in the last lunar month, the time of pilgrimage, the soul reaches the object of its desire, the Kaaba, the house of the Divine Beloved in Mecca, or else the mausoleum of the beloved Prophet in Medina. By this time the soul is finally no longer depicted as the longing *virahini*, but as a *wasli*, "one who has arrived [or has been united]." In the words of the *Bujh Niranjan*, she is like "sugar completely dissolved in water."

The connection between the Prophet and rain has its place in this context as well. The Quran describes Muhammad as "a mercy for the worlds" (Sura 21:107), and he appears in poetical parlance as a great rain cloud. This is due to the fact that rain in many Islamic areas is also called *rahma*, "grace, mercy." Thus, in Shah ʿAbdul Latif's *Sur Sarang* we read:

> My Beloved has put on
> his gown of clouds today!

The Prophet's benevolence revives the withered soul in much the same way rain revives the arid fields. Difficult to determine is just how great an influence the *barahmasa* rain symbolism has exerted here.

The Ismaili *ginans* bear witness to a further development of the motif of the longed-for groom of the bride-soul. These religious songs depict the imam (the secular and spiritual leader of the community known today as the Aga Khan) as the passionately desired beloved. This idea dates back to the Middle Ages and, as Ali S. Asani has recently shown, it continues to animate the poetry of the Ismaili community today.

The mystical songs of the Sindhi Sufis were frequently collated into *surs*, or "chapters," each one of which was named after its melody. Ever since the days of Shah Mian

'Inat in the early eighteenth century, works so arranged
were described as *Risalo*. Indeed, this whole corpus of lyric
love poems was meant to be sung, not read; nor were they
to be used as a grammatical quarry for pedantic philolo-
gists. This is one of the reasons why they are so repetitious.
Eight or more verses frequently begin with the same for-
mula, and it does not change much as the poem goes on.
Even the subsequent verses, which more often than not are
held together with internal rhyme, evince only slight variations, rather like small ripples on the surface of a pond. The
songs devoted to a specific main theme end with a *kafi* or a
way. This is a lyric poem usually sung by a chorus; over
time it has come to take on an independence all its own.
The ecstatic verses of the Sindhi mystic Sachal Sarmast
(d. 1826) are good examples of this trend. He is very fond of
repeating the first line of the *kafi* or else of interpolating it
after every second line of verse.

In keeping with the nature of folk poetry, these verses res-
onate with alliteration and frequently defy both grammatical
analysis and literal translation. Even so, they continue to
delight the ear. The Sindhi language is exceptionally rich in
verbal expressions, an apparently inexhaustible source of
poetic embellishment.

These poets frequently include allusions to the Quran as
ways to comfort and console their heroines. Sayings of the
Prophet crop up here and there, and a well-read poet like
(the allegedly illiterate!) Shah 'Abdul Latif has also quoted
an Arabic proverb or a classical Arabic verse now and
again, regardless of the seeming absurdity that a Sindhi village maiden should have had any knowledge of Arabic
(apart, of course, from the few Quranic verses necessary for
prayer).

Historical accuracy was never a high priority in this
genre; the heroines exist beyond the boundaries of tempo-
ral and spatial history, for they are meant to be eternal
models of the absolute love of God. The same holds true for

place-names as well. Places familiar from the classical tradition are mixed up rather freely, especially in the Siraiki poetry of Khwaja Ghulam Farid.

But just who are the heroines of these stories? The poets assumed a familiarity with folktales on the part of their audiences and thus never bothered to include historical or geographical details in their songs. These stories, especially those of Shah ʿAbdul Latif, always begin *in media res*, as it were, which is to say, with one of the most dramatic moments. Once introduced, the tales develop in bits and pieces; they stop short here and there, make use of flashbacks and reminiscences, repeat themselves, and are for the most part oblivious of any logical sequence of events.

The Punjab has the story of Hir Ranjha, today close to a national epic. Hir, hailing from the region of Jhang (where the alleged mausoleum of this loving couple is located), falls in love with Ranjha, a member of the Sial clan, as she listens to the music of his flute. Nevertheless, her family marries her off to another man, whom she rejects. Pretending to have been bitten by a snake, she grants her beloved, now disguised as a dervish physician, entry to her rooms. New attempts to enter into a legitimate marriage with him are confounded by her family, and by one old uncle in particular. Hir dies. One version of the story has her poisoned; others leave her disowned and cast off.

Like other romantic love stories in India, this tale too is presumably based on historical fact, and it offers informative insights into the family structure and customs of the great Panjabi clans. Its poetic composition dates back to very early traditions. No fewer than a hundred versions exist in Panjabi, Urdu, Sindhi, and Persian, one of which the Sufi poet Afarin included in his Persian mathnawi *Naz u niyaz*, "Coquetry and Supplication" (ca. 1730). Allusions to Hir and Ranjha can even be found as early as the verses of Madho Lal Husain (d. 1593), the first known mystic composing poetry in his mother tongue, Panjabi.

And yet it is not the learned versions that have made this
story so famous but rather its popular folkloric renditions.
Hir represents the soul that loves God, personified in Ranjha, and a modern Panjabi is surely justified in (correctly)
interpreting every character in the tale allegorically. It is
primarily the ecstatic verses of Bullhe Shah, the minstrel
who died in Qasur in 1758, that repeatedly allude to the
unending love between Hir and her beloved, and his verses

> Repeating Ranjha, Ranjha in my mind,
> I myself have become Ranjha[4]

have entered the vernacular almost as a proverb since they
express the complete union of the lover and the beloved.
The epic poem of his slightly younger compatriot Warith
Shah is the most widely known of all Panjabi tales, and
Muslims and Hindus, peasants and scholars alike have
been and continue to be moved by its rhymes and melodies.

The story of Sassi Punhun seems to be older yet; it dates
as far back as 1643, when a Sindhi poet included it in a
Persian mathnawi under the title *Ziba Nigar.* Later Persian
versions were written by Muslims and Hindus (Jaswant Rai
Munshi [1728] and Lalla Janpraket), while the Rohilla
leader Mahabbat composed an Urdu mathnawi with the
title *Asrar-i mahabbat,* "The Secrets of Love" or of "Mahabbat" early in the nineteenth century.

The fate of Sassi and Punhun is common knowledge
throughout present-day Pakistan, for the story has been
used for literary purposes for a very long time. That
becomes evident from the fact that there are passing allusions to Bhambhore, the home of the loving Sassi, in Sindhi
literature of the sixteenth century. It was only in the great
Risalo of Shah ʿAbdul Latif, however, that the theme was
elaborated in great detail in five different *surs.* Cross-

---

4 Ibid., p. 152.

references to the Sassi cycle turn up again and again in other chapters as well, including *Ripa* and *Dahar*. The theme was obviously very close to the poet's heart.

The tale of Sohni Mehanwal was also known throughout the Pakistani flatland and can be described as an inverted Hero and Leander story. It originated on the shores of the Chenab. Muslims and Hindus alike revere Shah ʿAbdul Latif's *Risalo* almost as a sacred script. To its already familiar tales he added a number of events that occurred only in Sind. These include the moving story of Marui, the village maiden from the Thar Desert. And yet, while for him Sassi and Sohni become symbols of the soul that finally reaches its beloved in death after enduring the greatest hardships along the way, the lovesick Marui is the soul that never forgets her original home, no matter where she may be in the world.

These three traditional tales will be examined in greater detail in the next three chapters. Shah ʿAbdul Latif elaborated several other traditional tales as well, all based on events in Sindhi history: these include the ballads of Lila Chanesar and Nuri Tamachi, both of which date back to the fifteenth century. Another tale from the Thar (Momal Rano) and even a legend from Svarashtra (namely, the horrible story of King Dhyaj) occupied his attention as well. Their heroines can all pass as *nafs* symbols: Lila and Momal are typical representatives of the *nafs ammara* and turn into "scolding souls" through sorrow and separation. Nuri, on the other hand, is the "soul at peace," who is warmly accepted by her beloved.

The story of Lila Chanesar takes place in the fifteenth century, when Jam Chanesar was prince in Sind. He and his wife, Lila, led a happily married life until another woman conceived an ardent desire for the king and hired herself out as maidservant in the royal palace. One day she showed Lila an extremely precious diamond necklace, *naulakʰha*, "worth 900,000 gold pieces." (Tradition has it that this is the highest possible value of any piece of jewelry.) Lila would gladly have acquired it, but the deceptive servant was loath to sell it. She had but one wish, and that was to spend a night with Chanesar. Blinded by avarice, Lila agreed, but when the king awoke from his intoxicated slumbers the next morning, he discovered the deception and banished his foolish wife. She spent the following years in misery and regret until, completely purified, she was once again allowed to approach her beloved:

> Blinded by the diamond's gleam,
> She stumbled, shattered by pride.
> Others came to her and cried:
>> O Shame! and they cried and cried against her.
> They burned and singed her heart
>> With scorn and ridicule.
>> The wretched woman soon forgot
> The joys of her youth.

The foolish, evil-inciting soul squandered her first and only beloved for glittery and worldly goods. Having succumbed to material temptations, Lila was obliged to endure unending sorrow and suffering before she was once again accepted by her forgiving beloved. The tale ends with her dying at his feet.

The sensuously beautiful, "man-killing" Momal also belongs in this group. She becomes the beloved of Prince Rano, who, captivated by her charms, travels far distances every night to be by her side. One night he happens to be delayed; in the meantime she has dressed her sister up as a man. When he finally does arrive, Rano finds his beloved apparently in the arms of another. Once again the result is separation—after all, one does not flirt with love, nor try, even in jest, to deceive one's only beloved. Like Lila, Momal turns penitent and passes her days and nights in constant remorse. She thus purifies her soul and ultimately realizes that her heart is filled with Rano's presence—nothing else exists except the splendor of his beauty. Rumi's son, Sultan Walad, writes in his poetic biography of his father that the latter discovered his mystical beloved Shams-i Tabrizi "radiant as the moon" within himself. The verses that Shah ʿAbdul Latif puts in the mouth of Momal express the same identification between lover and beloved, between the perfectly purified, mirror-like soul and the radiant friend:

> Where shall I guide my camel?
>> The light of the moon has flooded the landscape!
> I bear Kaak's chamber within me,
>> Within me his abode, his countenance—
>> Of all most Beloved!
> There is none else but he.
>
> Where shall I guide my camel?
>> The light of the moon has flooded the landscape!
> I bear Kaak's chamber within me,
>> Spring's verdant groves and vales—
>> I see my Friend in everything,
> There is no other sound or name.

Only once, however, does the heroine appear not as a seeking, striving, penitent woman but rather as one who has already attained the blissful, satisfying state of *nafs mutmaʾinna*, the soul at peace, when she is finally called home by her Lord. This story is sung in the *kamod* melody, the tune usually played during the early afternoon rest period while the large, typically Sindhi beds swing gently back and forth.

Jam Tamachi, a wealthy Sindhi prince of the fifteenth century, falls in love with the fishermaid Nuri. She accompanies him wherever he goes, always wondering why the mighty king has chosen her of all people. After all, she is a poor, miserable, casteless girl who smells of fish, whereas his palace is home to the most beautiful and richest of all princesses. Not surprisingly, this absolute humility and devotion on the part of the maiden are what the king finds

so appealing. Through his love for the fishermaid, Jam
Tamachi becomes the "slave of his slave" in much the same
way that the Persian tradition tells of Sultan Mahmud of
Ghazna, who loved his Turkish slave Ayaz so intensely that
their roles seemed to be reversed. In Rumi's *Mathnawi*,
Ayaz reminds himself again and again of how poor and miserable he was before the Sultan chose him above all others
and showered him with kindness. In Shah ʿAbdul Latif's
tale, Nuri too is constantly praising the generosity and
kindness of the prince, the Omni-Affluent, and the words
the poet puts in the mouth of the fishermaid in praise of the
king show more clearly than anything else that the identification between Tamachi and God is appropriate, for his
throne manifests *kibriya*, the Glory of God (II.10). Even the
Quranic description of the One and Unique God in Sura
112, "He begot none nor is He begotten," is used with
regard to Nuri's noble beloved. These exemplary individuals
notwithstanding, Shah ʿAbdul Latif's favorite heroines are
Sassi, Sohni, and Marui, for their stories are paradigms of
the mystical life.

⟵ 10 · Sassi's Wanderings ⟶

T HE STORY OF SASSI, the "Moon-like One," is part of the narrative tradition of Sind and the Panjab and, like all folk tales, is preserved in many different variations. The basic plot lines, and the ones Shah ᶜAbdul Latif followed in the versions he included in his *Risalo*, are these:

A daughter is born to a brahman, and her horoscope foretells her marriage to a Muslim. In order to avert this ignominy, she was put in a basket and set afloat in the river. A Muslim washerman's family in Bhambhore finds her and raises her as if she were their own. The child develops into such a beauty that admirers and suitors come from far away just to catch a glimpse of her. Even Punhun, the prince of Kecch—the region where the mountains of Balochistan sink into the Indus Valley—sets out for Bhambhore. After many adventures immaterial to the mystical interpretation of the story and therefore not mentioned by Shah ᶜAbdul Latif, Punhun reaches his goal, falls in love with Sassi and stays with her. His highborn relatives are understandably horrified that the prince has become a washerman—one of the lowest castes! They turn up in Bhambhore, intoxicate the pair, and abduct Punhun from their common abode. When Sassi awakens, she discovers that the bed is empty and the guests' camels have long since departed, carrying the sleeping Punhun away with them.

This is the point at which Shah ʿAbdul Latif begins his tale. In her desperation, the abandoned woman leaves everything behind and sets out to find her beloved. Remorse goads the soul on to abandon the world and everything in it, to set out on her journey. Remorse is the first step along the mystical path, and once a person sets out on it she may never look back to the world again. Naturally, Sassi is unable to catch up with the swift camels of the Baluchis, and after many adventures in the wilderness she passes away. According to one version, Sassi is harassed by a shepherd and dies; Punhun, who has set out to look for her, falls dead at her grave, thus effecting their ultimate union in death. Shah ʿAbdul Latif, however, leaves the ending open, as is his wont.

Just how important the theme of the wandering woman was for Shah ʿAbdul Latif can be seen in the various different keys he uses to tell his tale. A specific key or pitch is ordinarily reserved for each individual female figure as well as for each general theme, but the story of Sassi is composed in the melodic forms of *Sassi Abri,* "the weak one," *Maʿdhuri,* "the miserable one," *Desi,* "native," *Khohyari,* "connected to the mountains," as well as in the *Husaini* melody, which is usually reserved for lamentations, as in the songs dedicated to the memory of the Prophet's grandson Husain, who was killed at Kerbela. Like Husain, Sassi too is a martyr. Other chapters of the *Risalo* contain repeated allusions to her fate as well as references to her sufferings.

In fact, she seems to have been a familiar soul symbol from very early times. The verses of Shah ʿAbdul Latif's great-grandfather Shah ʿAbdul Karim (d. 1694) already contain the observation:

> No one has yet managed to take from Bhambhore
> two things together:
> A yearning for one's Beloved
> and ties to the material world.

And didn't classical love mystics, like Ahmad Ghazzali (d. 1126), say:

> On the path of true monotheism
> You can not follow two directions in prayer.
> One seeks either the satisfaction of the Friend
> or one's own desire!

The one who leaves her worldly home to search for the beloved must no longer cling to secular values, to ephemeral possessions. Sassi's fate echoes throughout the verses of later poets and can still be heard today.

The chapter called *Sassi Abri* begins with the words: "My first and last wish is to travel to my Beloved. . . ." Shah ʿAbdul Latif follows Sassi and eavesdrops on how she relives the events of the past weeks again and again during her wanderings through the deserts and mountains. He hears her grieve as she recalls the days she shared with her beloved. In her mind's eye she relives the arrival of Punhun's caravan:

> *Kechan ayo qafila,*
> From Kecch there came a camelcade.

She remembers how glorious this caravan was, how beautiful even the prince's companions were. The washermaiden admired these men back then. Of course she knew that Punhun was the son of a king while she was only a girl of the lower caste:

> He is used to the fragrance of musk
> and I to the smell of soap.

His scent perfumed the marketplace, for as a true lord he naturally emanated the loveliest fragrances that delight both heart and soul. She recalls his scent (scent is, after all, a medium of memory) and invents ever-new descriptions of her own miserable state. Is not her hair in the hands of the Baluchis? Which is to say, she has fallen for them, completely and absolutely. And, as she wanders through the dusty steppes, she yearns to rub the dust from her beloved's arms all over her own body.

Sassi knew that Punhun loved her very dearly and had even become a washerman in order to be near her; but she also knew that his family was against the union. Thus she sighs:

> Would that no one in Kecch even knew
> of my unhonorable caste,
> Then Punhun need not be ashamed
> when he thinks of my people.

But now she's being punished because she stretched her feet across the bed. This is the way the soul that has set out on the path of perfection constantly rebukes itself for not remaining alert. *Qillat al-manam*, "little sleep," is one of the fundamental rules of the Sufi path. The poet, who occasionally assumes an admonishing role, thus says reproachfully: "It was wrong for you to sleep when he went away."

The early women ascetics in Basra and Syria had already warned against this natural inclination of the body: "The grave is the place for sleep!" was their contention.

Even if Sassi's actual sin lay solely in her inattentiveness, she still must repent, because whoever succumbs to the "sleep of heedlessness" instead of concentrating completely on the beloved must pay dearly for this forgetting of God, until, through constant castigation and remorse, she finally becomes the *nafs lawwama*, the reprimanding soul. This is why the poet spurs Sassi on in her journeys and enjoins her to forget Bhambhore, the "world," until she finally exclaims: "I will set fire to Bhambhore!" Everything having anything to do with earthly existence has to be annihilated so that nothing remains but the search for the beloved.

Clearly, Sassi's wanderings can also be seen as an inner journey projected outward. This is why the poet's warning voice finds ever new ways to remind us that the beloved cannot be found by simply wandering from country to country. Instead, the seeker must sit quietly in one place and "roast" which is to say, submit to the purification that comes through ascetic living and meditation.

The theme of the inner journey is a favorite of most mystics. When at the end of his great travel poem Maulana Rumi sings

> You lack a foot to travel?
> Then journey into yourself—
> That leads to transformation
> of dust into pure gold!

he is picking up on the thoughts of his predecessors in the Persian world. Half a century before him ʿAttar described the migration of the thirty birds to Simurgh, the bird king, where, at the end of their arduous journey through seven valleys, they realize their own identity with the Divine Bird. In his *Musibatnama,* ʿAttar describes the inner journey of the soul during the forty days of seclusion. This journey ends with the wayfarer finding the Divine Beloved in the ocean of his own soul. In fact, the true seeker is only traversing the expanses of the soul; as the Egyptian mystic Ibn ʿAta Allah (d. 1309) summarized a full century after ʿAttar:

> If it weren't for the wide fields of the soul,
> there would be no real journey for the wanderer,
> for there are no distances between you and Him
> that your travels could overcome,
> and no separation between you and Him
> that your arrival could erase.

Sassi, roaming through the wilderness, knows that she has violated the law of love because she slept instead of staying awake at the side of her beloved. Not only that: she also neglected to tie the visitors' camels in such a way that they could not steal away silently into the night.

> If you had bound their knees with your hair,
> you would not have had to bear
> the swaying of the departing beasts.

The desert is scorchingly hot, and Sassi wanders about in a double inferno, that of the day and that of the fire of separation, just like a yogini whose ascetic exercises sometimes included sitting on the ground surrounded by four fires in the height of summer. In his *Sur Desi*, Shah ʿAbdul Latif weaves two appropriate Arabic sayings into his text: "The journey is a stretch of hellfire" and "Love is the fire set by God." Caught up in this situation, Sassi recalls how, sitting at her spinning wheel in Bhambhore, she was unable to finish her work because the blood-drenched tears that fell from her eyes soiled both her gown and the spinning wheel. That's why she abandoned both gown and wheel and set out on her journey, on the "terrible path of God," as Rumi once called it, in search of her beloved. But she sees with horror that the sun is already sinking, and her hope of finding Punhun before nightfall comes to naught:

> The sun is sinking behind the trees,
> and dusk discharged its bloody beams—
> Oh, I am defeated, Mother!
> for now darkness is falling.
>
> The sun is sinking behind the trees,
> lending darkness to the evening shades.
> The ones who've absconded with my spouse
> are already beyond the mountain range.
>
> The sun is sinking behind the trees
> while the rising mist of dusk turned red.
> Oh, Mother! I have been killed
> in this darkness.

She is lonely, but knows that her girlfriends and companions would never have been able to undertake such a journey:

> Would that my companion does not
> follow me to the desert!
> So far from water, so long the path,
>   all steppes and stones and dust.
>   If she would perish from the pangs of thirst
> she would curse the Beloved . . .

No, her companions in the village will criticize her, but how could they possibly understand that the beautiful, desirable Sassi is willing to give up everything to wander about through deserts and mountains, always in search of her lost beloved? —For her girlfriends have not been struck by the beam of eternal beauty and thus have no conception of unconditional love.

> Oh had they but seen the Friend
>   with their eyes as I have with mine—
> they would cry out: "Go! Find him!"
>   They would plunge into the mountains.
>
> But they haven't seen the Friend,
> may scorn not smite them, the dear ones,
>   for they would cry out loud, like me,
>   and would bite their hands in remorse.

This theme turns up a number of times in mystical folk poetry, for only he "who has beheld beauty with his eyes" can truly understand the state of the loving soul. Even the *Bujh Niranjan* says:

> Without the Lord this woman is desolate,
> she weeps the whole day long for her Beloved.
> Father, mother—no one understands her,
> for only he who has been smitten can empathize. (19/2)

We might add that Sassi, to a certain extent, is the feminine counterpart of Majnun, who, lost in thoughts of his Laila, roamed about the desert, even though his beloved was nowhere near as attractive to other men as she was to him: "Only Majnun's eyes can see Laila's beauty!"

> Her love for Punhun gives meaning to Sassi's life,
>> and she exclaims:
> Wandering about in search of Punhun
> is my one and only joy.

The physical body has no significance whatsoever on this journey, and material goods would be merely a hindrance. Only those who have left all worldly possessions behind are able to travel the difficult path, for one has to be naked to reach Kecch. Whoever is burdened with the material things of daily life and remains in his village will never appreciate the beauty of the Friend, for "nothing can be compared with Him," as the Quran says (Sura 42:11), and "even if you have a hundred thousand friends, none can compare with Punhun!" The beauty of the beloved is incomparable; he is "like the earth's green garb," and

> Bright and motley
> is the Beloved, like silk.
> How could one ever forget him
> who intoxicates the soul?

Employing another popular allusion in Islamic mysticism, Shah ʿAbdul Latif says that one has to lay the sword of *la*, "no, not," on the throat of the lower soul, that is, of the base instincts. In its graphic—which is to say its written—form the first half of the profession of faith, *la ilaha illa ʿLlah*, "There is no god but God," can be said to resemble a scimitar to a certain extent. As such it can serve as a warning to the seeker that everything that seems to have existence outside God, everything that threatens to divert attention from God, must be sacrificed so that only He, the One without peer, remains before the eyes of the seeker.

These are the thoughts that accompany Sassi in her wanderings through the mountains, borne on by her love alone:

> Though the day be hot,
> keep going, keep going on!

> Primordial love has bound you
> to the Baluchi.
> Glow like cinders your whole life long,
> for no place is free of pain—
> run on through heat and cold:
> You've no time to waste.

> Make haste, through summer's heat
> and winter's chill,
> There is no time to rest.
> Once darkness descends and overcomes you,
> you'll lose sight of his tracks again.

It almost seems as if the stones of the threatening peaks of Pabb were Sassi's only trousseau: she had nothing else to bring to her beloved.

And yet Sassi sometimes abandons all hope, because the genuinely loving woman is not supposed to have a mind for the morrow. The true Sufi is the *ibn ul-waqt*, the "son of the moment," of that instant where for a moment he is struck out of the serial time that came into being with creation by the eternal now of divine time. The beginning of Rumi's *Mathnawi* says: "Talk of tomorrow is not one of the conditions of the path."

Shah ʿAbdul Latif uses yet another description of the grieving Sassi to lead his audience (or today: his readers) back to Rumi, for he compares her yearning for her Beloved to the wails of a lamenting flute. It is the flute and its sound that Rumi invokes in the first lines of his *Mathnawi*:

> Hearken to the reed, how it tells its tale
> and bemoans the pain of separation:
> "Ever since I was cut from my native reed-bed
> all the world weeps when it hears my song."

Like this flute, Sassi too weeps in recollection of the time she spent together with her beloved. Sassi sometimes even scolds the mountains for being so hard and for cutting her

feet; at other times, though, they are dear to her again, simply because her beloved wandered through them. And yet
never before in her life had she seen such jungles, devoid of
water and crawling with blue snakes. Even the birds in such
a place despair, for "every mountain is an elephant in
strength and grandeur." Of course, the wandering seeker is
comforted by the Quranic message that "patience is comely"
(Sura 12:18, 83), but she is sometimes close to desperation
because there is no end of suffering. She wishes the separation from her beloved hadn't been written on the pre-eternal
tablet and thus wasn't inevitable:

> Had I had the slightest intimation
> that I would some day be struck by separation,
> I would have erased the words of Fate
>   from the pre-eternal tablet;
>   then I probably would not have experienced
> such torments on this endless path!

But there is no way out:

> When so and so many hours are written on the
>   Tablet of Fate,
> that many and no fewer must pass!

And the one whom fate has determined a seeker must set
out on the most difficult paths without any expectation of
respite:

> Such were the paths that Sassi pursued—
> paths that would have cost heroes their lives!
> The towering mountains are as flat as the steppes
> to the mind and eye of love.

That may very well be true, but it doesn't alter the fact
that the despairing soul still calls for her beloved, still
yearns to see him, to share his very vitality; and all because
she is confused and powerless. She thinks she hears the
dogs of Kecch barking, but while the dogs chew their bones,
"the true God-seeker," the courageous young hero, "eats his

liver," which is just another way of saying that he endures unutterable torment. Yes, Sassi would gladly tear the flesh from her shoulders and cast it to the wild beasts or even offer it as food for the crows:

> Would that the crows of Kecch
> might pluck and feast on my flesh!

Since the crow is the messenger bird, the loving Sassi cries out:

> *kare kang kornishun,*
> Bring him greetings, O crow,
> fall prostrate at the feet of my Beloved,
> and don't drop the message I give you
> somewhere along the way!

Were it up to her, Sassi would prefer to offer the crow from Kecch her heart for food. Indeed, the bird could eat her whole body with the single exception of her eyes, "for they have seen my Love" and are therefore holy. And yet even this is not complete devotion! Sassi would fain tear her own eyes out and toss them to the crows. After all, of what use are they to her if they should behold something other than her beloved? No, the lover doesn't need physical sight when she gazes upon her beloved with the eyes of her soul. (This sentiment is reminiscent of the Persian expression of being "jealous of one's own eyes.") Isn't the worldly eye a veil between the soul and its beloved, a foreign element that, in the end, is totally superfluous? As the women ascetics of the early days, "the weepers who let [others] weep," thought, it's better to weep oneself blind than to continue to see, for only then can the inner eye behold the beauty of the beloved. This thought is particularly characteristic of Ahmad Ghazzali.

But we still haven't had enough of the repetitions and horrible descriptions of the loving soul. In her desperation, Sassi climbs to the top of the trees to offer herself as food for the

vultures, and she does so as if she were ascending the gallows. "The gallows is the marriage bed," says Shah ʿAbdul
Latif when praising the martyred mystic al-Hallaj, whom
death united with his Eternal Beloved. As a martyr for Divine
Love, Hallaj has served the Sufis as a model ever since his
execution in 922. Sassi becomes a martyr of love in much the
same way. Legend has it that, during a dream, Hallaj's friend
asked God why He let Hallaj, the one who loved Him so very
much, be killed, and the answer he received was this: "He
who dies for love of Me, for him shall I be blood money." Shah
ʿAbdul Latif applies these exact words to Sassi too, thus ele-
vating her to the ranks of the "men of God" who endured
martyrdom for the sake of their love.

Sassi becomes weaker and weaker. Her one tonic is her
beloved. He sacrificed her like a poor little goat, to be sure,
but in becoming a *qurbani*, a sacrificial animal, she could
also hope to become a *qaribani*, one of the "close ones," for
she knows that the spiritual leader (who often represents
the Divine Beloved) first "boils and roasts" the seeker and
ultimately shows his mercy only after the rough or raw one
has ripened or matured. Rumi's influence can be seen here
again, for the "cooking" theme was a favorite of his long
before Lévi-Strauss made the opposition between the "raw
and the cooked" so famous. The fire of love matures the
seeker through pain and suffering:

> The fire called "separation" cooks the raw one
> and frees him from all hypocrisy . . .

That's the way Rumi puts it in his tale about the man who
continues to say "I" in the presence of his beloved. But the
most famous application of the cooking motif in Rumi's
works is by far the tale of the chickpeas. These become
edible only after being cooked, for only then can they play
their part in the life cycle of mankind by providing nourish-
ment, even though they initially try to jump out of the boiling water to escape the pain. Man, too, is supposed to turn

into a sweet morsel for love's consumption. This is why Sassi has to be "cooked" for long periods of pain; before she is ripe enough to reach her beloved she has to "empty" herself of all worldly contaminants.

Shah ʿAbdul Latif has yet another image to symbolize the seeker's torment:

> He first submerges him in bleach
> before dipping him in color.

In other words, the Divine Beloved cleanses the lover of every tie to the motley world, and this kind of purification is effected by means of caustic bleaching agents. After that, though, the person is dipped into the *sibghat Allah* (Sura 2:138), the "coloring of God," which to the mystic and poet means the absolute monotonal coloring of Divine Oneness:

> God the Lord, He is a dyer—
> all colors inhere in Him.

The beloved (in this context the spiritual leader as representative of God) was at times even presented as a washerman who thoroughly mishandled the laundry in order to clean it. Only those who have watched the Indian *dhobis*, the washers, pound and slap and strike their clothes against the stones as hard as they can, almost as if they wanted to break the stones apart, can understand just how pertinent this image really is.

Since the lover knows that all the torments the beloved sends are meant but to purify him, he perceives them as good fortune and happiness. This is why Sassi too desires nothing other than to wander about eternally. As long as the lover seeks the beloved, he carries Him in his heart; but if he has found Him, he would see Him with his eyes, and that, as the loving soul knows, would be but another obstacle: "the greater torment of Love fulfilled." (T. S. Eliot)

> Thus Sassi sings:
> He who asks will receive,

will see his Beloved.
He who seeks will arrive
at the Gate of Wonder.

You who seek should go ahead
for this is no earthly quest—
the Friend is never far
from the wandering seeker's heart.

The search is all I want, the search!
May I never find my Friend!
May this yearning in my soul
never be quenched by attaining its goal!

The search is all I want, I do not pine
for companions of days gone by;
having carried their burdens onward,
they set out for distant lands.

I search—and may I never find!
Beloved, you are so far away!
May my heart never find peace,
may my body never know rest.
I seek, and may I never find!
Yield to the voice of the lovers!
In this love, my Beloved,
lies the negation of my life.
May I rise up in peace in time for our union
on the Day of Judgment!

The goal, so it appears, is the path, the journey itself. The interminable yearning inherent in mankind ends perhaps only in death, although the Sufis also knew that a new journey begins the moment the Divine Beloved is found. Only now it is the indescribable journey into the immeasurable abysses of God.

Shah ʿAbdul Latif teaches his heroine the old Sufi motto: "Die, before ye die," for she must learn that "they who die before they die do not die when they die." Whoever overcomes his worldly existence through daily self-sacrifice, whoever conquers his lower instincts in the greater Holy War, whoever sacrifices his material desires, whoever leaves Bhambhore with the sole intention of following his beloved —this is the person who will be granted honor in eternal life.

Sassi's path seems to have no end. Many are the times she is completely exhausted, and all of nature shares in her suffering. Birds scream for sorrow; wild beasts succumb to grief when they see how the brave lover bears her afflictions; even the desert weeps. How can one person endure so much?

On the other hand, Sassi would have been unable to bear these torments and to maintain her equanimity, as it were, in her search if Punhun hadn't also been pining for her. With a verse once again taken from Rumi's *Mathnawi* (M I 1704) and translated almost literally, Shah ʿAbdul Latif alludes to the deepest mystery of all: that of the love between God and man:

> Not only the thirsty seek the water—
> the water seeks the thirsty as well.[1]

If God had not planted love in the heart of man simply because He loved him, man could not set out on the path of love at all—at least this is the way the Sufis interpret the concluding words of Sura 5:59: "He loves them and they love Him." Without the preexisting love of the Divine Master, no soul would be capable of love.

One need not necessarily head for the hills for the sake of the Beloved; the body itself is wilderness enough. Toward the end of *Sur Abri*, the most significant chapter in the Sassi cycle, Shah ʿAbdul Latif returns to the theme of the inner journey. The seeker is admonished to draw the veil of the self aside, for then she will see the beloved in her heart. The lover and the beloved are, in reality, one and the same.

---

[1] Quoted in Annemarie Schimmel, *Mystical Dimensions of Islam* (Chapel Hill, N.C., 1975), p. 392.

"Whoever knows himself becomes Punhun," is the way the poet puts it in a slightly altered rendition of the Arabic saying so popular among Sufi circles: "He who knows himself knows his Lord." Shah ʿAbdul Latif even goes a step farther in saying that this person actually *becomes* his beloved master.

When the loving Sassi, physically weak and helpless, burned by the scorching sun and parching wind, is on the very verge of union, the Angel of Death appears to her as a messenger from her beloved, and she learns that "to die along the path is supreme happiness."

Didn't the early Sufis repeatedly allude to the fact that death was beautiful, "for it joins the lover with his Beloved?" Over and over again Rumi passionately admonished his listeners not to grieve when his bier should be lowered into the grave: "A curtain is it for eternal bliss!"

For the pious, the day one dies is indeed an ʿurs, a wedding, when the longing soul will finally unite with its beloved: "Beautiful One, after death you shall come to Punhun" is the consolation Shah ʿAbdul Latif leaves with his seeker.

Perhaps the most poignant scene in the entire Sassi cycle comes toward the end of *Sur Maʿdhuri*, when Shah ʿAbdul Latif describes how the seeker senses the imminence of death and realizes that she has been separated from her beloved for thousands of days already. Once again she sings of her love, her sorrow, but by this time she has been totally transformed into love itself. She has reached the mystic's goal, she has herself become pure love. Such a love, however, knows no more separation between lover and beloved; instead, it embraces them both in a new unity. That which is human is completely subsumed in the Divine, for love is the innermost essence of God. What the great mystic thinkers like Ahmad Ghazzali and ʿAinul Qudat Hamadani, like Ruzbihan Baqli and all the medieval love mystics indicated and hinted at in precious sentences, the Sindhi poet says in a perfectly unpretentious way. It is the transformation of the loving soul at the end of its wanderings, when it is nothing other than love itself:

> Oh voice in the steppes:
>> as if the cuckoo were calling;
>> a lamentation and a sorrow:
> it is the Ah! of love.

> Oh voice in the steppes,
>> as if it were the parakeet's screech;
>> it is the wail of longing,
> it is the Ah! of love.

> Oh voice in the steppes,
>> as if the wild goose were honking—
>> cries from the depths of the sea—
> it is the Ah! of love.

> Oh voice in the steppes,
>> like the fiddle's melody;
>> it is the song of love,
> but common folk thought it was a woman's song.

⟋ 11 · Sohni Mehanwal ⟍

THE STORY OF SASSI, "who died on the path," as well as that of Sohni, "who died by drowning," can be traced back to the common heritage of the Panjab and the Indus Valley. Originally located in the region around the Chenab River, the tale of Sohni was transformed by Shah ʿAbdul Latif into a Sindhi legend.

Returning home from a journey, the noble and wealthy Mehanwal (Mehar) comes to a potters' village, falls in love with Sohni, the beautiful daughter of the master potter, and spends his whole fortune on pottery and earthenware. In order to stay near Sohni, he eventually hires himself out as a buffalo herdsman to Sohni's father. The girl, who is immediately married off to a man she doesn't love, swims across the river every night to the island where Mehanwal keeps his herds. A large jug of baked potter's clay serves as a kind of life jacket. Her sister-in-law suspects something and soon exchanges a jug of unbaked potter's clay for the baked one. Naturally, the substituted jug dissolves in the water and Sohni drowns. That means the Hero-and-Leander motif is reversed, for here too the active protagonist is a loving woman.

The swirling current or torrent that tears everything away in its wake is an ancient motif in oriental poetry, but this theme is especially real in the Punjab and in the Indus Valley, where the summertime floods following the thaw in the Himalayas and the Karakorum Range inundate the land with enormous force. Shah ʿAbdul Latif thus begins his tale with a reference to the river theme, to water. The river may be extremely powerful, but what the loving soul yearns for is precisely to sink down and be absorbed in its absolute oneness. To step into water means to take on a new life, even if the path toward that new life leads through death.

> The current is swift, the river is strong,
> yet, where love abides, the current is weak.
> He who loves the abyss
> dreams of nothing other than oneness.

Sohni wonders whether a person can resist the power of love at all—if her companions had but seen Mehar, they too would have grasped earthenware jugs in order to swim to him. This is exactly the way Sassi thinks about her girlfriends. The poet comforts Sohni with words that were popular among Indian Sufi circles ever since the thirteenth century: "He who seeks the Lord is a man." In this way, then, she too becomes a true "man of God," despite her biological gender.

The soul may sometimes falter and fail in the swirl of the current, but Shah ʿAbdul Latif reminds Sohni of the Quranic verse: "Do not despair of the mercy of God" (Sura 39:62). The breaking of her jug has a deeper meaning, for it represents the dissolution of all secondary causes, all worldly ties. This is a common theme in Islamic mysticism, but there are thousands of examples of the use of the word *shikast*, "breaking," in the Indo-Persian and Urdu poetry of the sixteenth to the nineteenth century as well. Even Ghalib (1797–1869) exclaims: "I am the sound of my own breaking." To be broken is a prerequisite for a new beginning. In verses that may have inspired Shah ʿAbdul Latif, Maulana Rumi said the weak vessel called "man" will be dashed to pieces when the wave of *alast*, the Divine Word to

mankind in the primordial covenant, overwhelms it, when
the heart recalls how the Creator said to it in pre-eternity:
"Am I not your Lord?" (Sura 7:172). When the individual
suddenly remembers his primordial tie to God, his Lord
and Beloved, he is obliterated and returns for a blessed
instant to the state "where he is as he was before he was,"
as Junaid, the leading mystic of Baghdad (d. 910), once
expressed it.

Sohni's jug must shatter so that worldly ties no longer
separate her from her Divine Beloved:

> Do not bring yourself with you
> and do not seek external support:
> the Beloved will belong to those
> who are led by love alone.

The first chapter sets the tone, so to speak, and it ends
with a comforting song in which Sohni is promised that
those who thirst after love will finally come to drink a "pure
beverage" (Sura 76:21)—the draft of Divine Grace and Love
promised to the believers in Paradise. And now the actual
story begins. As always, Shah ʿAbdul Latif begins his tale
with the climax. Sohni notices that the jug is dissolving and
that she cannot swim on. In desperation she calls to her
distant beloved, here as elsewhere called *Sahar* (for the
loved ones in these stories are given ever new names, as the
Divine Beloved possesses the "most beautiful names").

> In the terrible tumult of the tide,
>   where the din of fear dashed me down,
> in the midst of menacing forces:
>   what happened to the earthenware jug?
>   Oh Sahar, Ruler most wise—
> so helpless did I become on my path!
>
> In the terrible tumult of the tide
>   the mighty crocodiles,
> powerful alligators gathered beyond number
>   in the stream—

> my body has lost its strength,
>> separated as I am from you, Oh companion!
>> Prince! Sahar! Grant, Oh noble one, that
> I might reach my goal!

> In the terrible tumult of the tide,
>> where the eddies gurgle and swirl,
> bobbing between the beasts, I am
>> surrounded by enemies!
> Have mercy, Beloved! Out of love for me
>> pull your friend out of this flood;
>> stretch out your hand from beyond
> and save me from this abyss!

But this fit of desperation that Sohni experiences in a moment of apparent abandonment by God passes. Of course she knows it was wrong to leave her legitimate husband and go to her beloved. Such an act is sinful according to legal as well as personal standards of morality, and it sometimes happens that orthodox audiences express their disapproval of Sohni's behavior in disparaging and deprecatory terms! But isn't a part of love exactly that, to despise all worldly ties, all "normal" behavior, and expose oneself to the censure of the group? "Love is the abandonment of shame" says an ancient Sufi proverb, and Sohni says the same through the mouth of Shah ʿAbdul Latif:

> Reason, religion and shame—
> love has conquered all three!

After all, the loving one, the loving soul, stands beyond the pale of external norms. Even Maulana Rumi, that respectable professor and *paterfamilias* who was torn from his normal life by his passionate mystical love for the wandering dervish Shams of Tabriz, repeatedly sang (with more than a note of astonishment) about how he was now learning dancing, music, and poetry instead of devoting himself to scholarship and piety.

Having totally abandoned herself to love, Sohni now hardly notices the current that had so recently terrified her:

> He who yearns for Sahar
> does not look for ferry or boat.
> To him who thirsts after love,
> the rivers are but steps to climb.

Shah ʿAbdul Latif now praises the courageous woman (here called Todi): she deserves more honor than all the others because she etched the *alif* and the *mim* into her heart. *Alif* is the first letter of the alphabet, the metaphor for God the One, thus the letter that encompasses the wisdom of the world as well as the wisdom of the four revealed books. The eastern as well as western Sufis sought ever-new ways to express this idea. Hafiz, for example, says that nothing but the *alif* of the shape of the Beloved is written on the tablet of the heart, and the Turkish poet Yunus Emre (died around 1321) is in tune with the Indo-Pakistani mystics when he says:

> The meaning of the four books
> lies in one *alif*.

The Sindhi and Panjabi folk poets entreat

> *Molla mār ma mun*
> *Molla*, don't beat me up,

in retribution for the fact that they have only learned the first letter of the alphabet. *Mim*, on the other hand, the letter *m*, is closely associated with the Prophet Muhammad, whose divine name is Ahmad. Shah ʿAbdul Latif's observation probably refers to the famous extra-Quranic saying that had been recited again and again throughout the eastern Islamic world ever since the twelfth century: God said "*Ana Ahmad bila mim*, I am Ahmad without the *m*, which is to say *Ahad*, One." Only one single letter, *m*, stands between God and his Messenger, and since the numerical

value of *m* is 40, this allegedly Divine Word was considered
a reference to the forty steps separating man from God. The
number 40 naturally also contains an allusion to the forty
days of seclusion the dervish observes in order to purify
himself. Finally, it is also the number used to designate
patience and perseverance or else preparation for a new
and better time.

By introducing this kind of alphabet riddle (and specifically the play on the *alif* and the *m*), Shah ʿAbdul Latif iden-
tifies Sohni as a genuine Sufi soul. As such she was to be
ever mindful that the seeker's journey leads from the
shariʿa, the broad highway of religious laws which all Muslims have to observe, to the *tariqa*, the mystical path or
route by which one may ultimately hope to gain spiritual
knowledge and thus come to divine truth. The loving soul
yearns for unveiled knowledge, the spiritual sight of the
beloved. If it has entered the *otaq*, the chamber of the Sovereign where the object of its longing sits in all His glory on
His throne, the soul will observe the mutually enhancing
virtues of "patience" and "gratitude," and will remain
absolutely silent lest any word reaches the external realm,
for the mystery of loving union may not be revealed under
any circumstances.

Sohni, the soul, knows all this, and thus has to follow her
route through the river, has to travel the path of total self-
renunciation. This is why the poet cries out admiringly:

> No hesitation kept Sohni from her purpose,
> her haste led her straight to the stream—
> the poor mother who bore such a child
> has good reason to be proud,
> and if you saw her father,
> you would probably love him too.

How could she hesitate? "Mehar is in her heart day and
night!" And while other girls eagerly submerge themselves

in a cool bath on hot summer days, Sohni jumps into the water even on icy winter nights.

Shah ʿAbdul Latif transforms Sohni's sighs and lamentations into poetry. The sound of the tinkling cowbells reminds her of her beloved. (This image may very well go back to the Prophet himself, for Muhammad used to compare the sound heralding the approach of a revelation to the sound of a bell; the bell brings news of one's beloved.)

The only thing that keeps the seeker alive is her constant thinking of her friend, for, as the Sufi knows from his *dhikr* exercises, remembering the Divine Beloved keeps the soul alert. Wasn't the very name of her beloved both food and drink for the loving Zulaikha, and didn't this heroine of Sindhi poetry "cling to it with both hands?" But where could the beloved be? Again and again He seems to hide from the seeker, whose only desire is to enter into his Sovereign's chamber. Borne aloft by this desire, Sohni dives once again into the river—only to learn that the jug is breaking apart.

She sinks in the whirling turbulence with "eyes and face turned toward the buffalo herdsman." "Verily he is far from sight, but his love is near." The Quran says: "no mortal eyes can see Him" (Sura 6:103), but it also states that He is "closer to man than his jugular vein" (Sura 50:16).

Sohni watches as the jug dissolves and learns the time-honored Sufi wisdom that true life lies in the losing of one's earthly existence. The reader is immediately reminded of the verses the martyred mystic Hallaj had written so many years before:

> Kill me, Oh my trustworthy friends,
> for in my being killed is my life.[1]

This poem frequently served the later mystics, Rumi per-

---

[1] Quoted in Annemarie Schimmel, *Mystical Dimensions of Islam* (Chapel Hill, N.C., 1975), p. 69.

haps more than any other, as the basis for their meditations. Out of it grew their knowledge of the constant "dying
before dying" as taught by the alleged word of the Prophet
"Die, before ye die." Each sacrifice of an individual part of
the human self, every "dying," leads to a new life on a
higher level. The seeker's whole life is nothing more than an
ascending sequence of death and rebirth, a constant climb
upward during which a person's lower human qualities are
replaced by higher, divine ones. This is the thought behind
the traditional Sufi adage: "Qualify yourself with the qualities of God." Therefore, so says Shah ʿAbdul Latif, the truly
loving one breaks not only his jug but himself as well, in
order to eventually satisfy his longing.

Sohni seems to resemble a fish that, unable to survive in
air, constantly wonders how it can drink the water. "The
fish is never sated by the sea," is the way Rumi put it in the
introductory verses of his *Mathnawi.*

Sohni lives on in the current that carries her to her
beloved, even if all outward appearances confirm her death.
She has become completely absorbed; she has experienced
in other words total "de-becoming," and what Rumi says of
Hallaj in his *Fihi ma fihi* applies equally to Sohni:

> Absorption is that state where one is no longer there, where
> one can make no further efforts on one's own, one ceases to
> act or to move and is completely submerged in water. Every
> deed one performs is not one's own, but that of the water. But
> when someone thrashes his hands and feet about in the
> water, one shouldn't call that absorption, or when he contin-
> ues to proclaim "Oh, I'm drowning!," that isn't true absorp-
> tion either.
>
>   Take this saying [*anaʿl-haqq*]: "I am the creative Truth."
> Many people consider this a great presumption, but to say "I
> am the creative Truth" is in fact a sign of extreme humility.
> To say "I am God's servant" is to make a false claim, for man
> is saying that two exist, one being himself, the other God. But
> when someone says: "I am God," that is, "I am nothing. He is

everything, nothing exists except God, I am completely and absolutely non-existent, I am nothing," then the humility is even greater.

Only he who manifests neither movement nor action nor deed and whose movements are nothing more than the movements of the water, only he has truly succumbed to the water.

This is the fate of the loving Sohni, for her love for Mehar is eternal. Her love existed the same way Sassi's love for Punhun did, the same way Marui's love for the Marus did ever since the days of the primordial covenant. The words *alastu bi-rabbikum*, "Am I not your Lord?" thus provide the keynote for a whole series of verses:

> The beauty of the Beloved existed
> long before our fates were sealed,
> long before the creative "Be!"
>> and every other word was spoken.
> Angels had not yet come to be
>> when Sohni's lamentations were heard,
>> when love bound her to her shepherd.
> So said the poet Latif.

> And when He asked the souls:
> "Am I not your Lord?"
> the eternal affirmation of "Yes, we attest it"
>> became a good omen in my heart.
> That's when I, undaunted, caught
>> hold of Mehar's love.
>> That I should have dared to follow him,
> Oh friends, that is my right!

How could she have turned away from Him, since her love for Him had already been written on the well-preserved Tablet? Surely many souls have sought the path to the Beloved One ever since the days of the primordial covenant, but they were shortsighted. They mistook the manifold waves of worldly phenomena for truth and let themselves be deceived and carried away by them; thus they lost sight of the real goal. Sohni, however, was blessed in that she did not succumb to the deceptive and changing forms of the world, but concentrated completely and absolutely on love instead. Her dive into the river was the decree of the Divine Beloved, and when He decrees something, no one can resist. His love draws the soul toward Him and gives it the strength to jump into the current—just as it was Punhun's longing for Sassi that enabled her to endure the hardships along the dangerous path through mountain and desert.

> In Sohni's experience
> black is the night and unbaked the jug,
> and no raft made of goatskin;
> and all for the sake of her Beloved
> no leisure and no rest.
> To Love the river seemed
> a dry and level road.

Granted, this loving soul did experience a momentary panic, but now the river seems dry to her. She drowns, of course, but only in the mortal sense, and Mehar begs the fishermen to cast their nets, all the while cursing the cruel river. This scene clearly reveals the ambivalent character of the beloved: on the one hand he is the weak, worldly friend everyone knows from the traditional narrative, while on the other he serves as symbol for the primordial beloved.

Sohni is the stronger of the two, for her mind is not directed toward the visible beloved, whom the Sufis used to call the "metaphorical beloved." Her love is undying; she transformed her heart into a mirror reflecting her friend. The lover, thoroughly purified by pain, has become a mirror and is thus closer to the beloved than he is to himself. This is the image the Sufis have often employed ever since the days of Ahmad Ghazzali (d. 1126).

Shah ʿAbdul Latif ends the story of the woman drowned

in the eternal ocean, the one who experienced total "de-becoming," with a profession of the oneness of all being. In doing so he alludes again to Hallaj, whom literary tradition frequently called by his father's name *Mansur*, "victorious one." Sassi's tale had already conjured up the image of this martyred mystic, and his fate is mirrored also in the image of the person completely submerged in water. But why was he the only one condemned for his *ana ʾl-haqq*? Doesn't every created thing proclaim: "I am the Truth?"

> Water, earth, river: a scream!
> Tree and bush: a lamentation.
> Everything was worthy
> of the gallows.
> Thousands of Mansurs—
> how many do you still want to hang?
>
> Wherever you look you sense
> the presence of the Friend, the Beloved;
> the whole earth is Mansur—
> how many do you want to kill?

The hundred thousand raiments of the waves seem to differ from one another only to the mortal eye, for the waters, the endless expanse of the ocean, are but one and the same. Whoever plumbs the depths, like Sohni, doesn't think about what she's doing any more. When drowning in the Divine Ocean, one forgets all intellectual exercises; there's no room for them during an ecstatic love experience. Rumi's *Mathnawi* hints at this truth in his tale about the haughty grammarian and the boatman. As the boat was sinking, the boatman taught the grammarian what was truly important: not grammar, *nahw*, but "de-becoming," *mahw* (M I 2838f.).

All yearning is now a thing of the past. The apparent turbulence of the waves, the foam and the swirling flood that managed to frighten Sohni in the beginning were now no longer perceptible to the loving soul, for it has been absorbed into the unfathomable abyss of the Divine Ocean.

Shah ʿAbdul Latif dedicates the end of this section of his poem to the exclusive praise of the sea, of that ocean of God's love in which Sohni "drowned" and in which she found her beloved in much the same way the seeker in ʿAttar's *Musibatnama* found the Divine Beloved in the ocean of his soul. How could such an ocean possibly have any boundaries or end?

> Yearning has no end,
> nor does love know any bounds.
> Love cannot be measured—
> it alone knows how great it is.

Sohni's fate is the clearest representation of "de-becoming" in water that has come down to us, but for a mystic who lived near the mighty Indus River, water symbolism was an obvious and very natural thing. Perhaps the most familiar chapter in his *Risalo*, and the one made famous by Allan Faqir's song, is *Samundi*, the "Song of the Sea." This tale tells of the fisherman's wife who longingly awaits her husband's return from a distant journey. She ties ribbons on trees as people still do when making a vow and pours perfume on the waves of the sea to ensure his healthy and happy return and in hopes that he will bring precious jewels or spices back home from Aden or Sri Lanka.

Here as in *Sur Srirag* (which echoes the terminology of the Sassi cycle), Shah ʿAbdul Latif culls his descriptions from the daily life of the Sindhi women whose husbands have to battle the dangerous river and sea. The brief *Sur Ghatu*, on the other hand, has as its theme the Sindhi story of little Morirro. Little Morirro kills the sea monster that had already taken the lives of all his brothers. As interesting as these chapters are from a folkloric point of view, the

actual theme of mystical experience is not as clearly
expressed in them as it is in the grand-scale descriptions of
the loving women who either perish in the wilderness or
drown in the river or who, like Marui, see in the wastes of
the Thar Desert their own long-lost and sorely missed
homeland.

◣ 12 · Omar Marui ◢

Both Sassi and Sohni try to reach the primordial beloved, the one via her wanderings through the wilderness, the other via her death-defying plunge into the river. But there are other woman-souls who pass their lives in patience, albeit burdened by an ever-deepening yearning. Imprisoned in this world, they are unable to effect their own return home and their reunion with their beloved. Suhrawardi, the Master of Illumination (killed in 1191), spoke of *ghurbat algharbiyya*, "western exile." Here the soul is enveloped in darkness and grief until it finally finds its way back home to the Orient of Lights, to the native soil of Yemen, to that source of happiness from whence the "fragrance of the breath of the Merciful One" once blew its way. To this group of symbols belong some of the most familiar images of oriental poetry: the falcon-soul imprisoned by the old woman "world"; the gazelle penned up in the cow stall; the captured elephant yearning for its native India which breaks its shackles after dreaming of its native land: "The elephant saw India in his dreams last night and broke loose his fetters—who had the strength to restrain him?" wonders Rumi.

In Shah ʿAbdul Latif's poetry, Marui is the representative of this yearning for home, the symbol of the homesick soul living in constant recollection of its native soil.

Marui is a girl from a village in the Thar Desert in the southeastern region of today's Pakistan. She loves her village and her people, the Marus, for they are her friends and relatives. Like so many other girls, she goes to the village fountain to fetch water. The mighty Omar hears of the girl's beauty and carries her off to his palace in Omarkot. He wants to win her affections and take her as a concubine, but Marui resists his every attempt at seduction. All she can think of is her homeland and "the first beloved." Realizing his defeat, the prince finally sends her back, but at a time when the rains had turned the desert into a lush and verdant green. According to one version of the tale, Marui is killed by her fellow tribesmen because they don't believe her assurances of innocence and purity. Shah ʿAbdul Latif, on the other hand, says nothing about her end: his theme revolves solely around yearning, recollection and the hope of return.

As in his other tales, the poet begins his *Sur Marui* in *media res* and leads his listeners to the palace in Omarkot, where the abducted girl is passing her time in solitude. During her imprisonment her thoughts constantly focus on memories of the primordial love she bears for the Marus. The plural form "Marus" is used here, as elsewhere, to denote the One True Beloved who manifests Himself in the most varied forms while still eluding all concrete description. Even Sassi's monologues repeatedly speak of the "Kecchans" when she means Punhun. This is just one of many linguistic peculiarities. [Saintly men, for instance, were often addressed and spoken about in the plural. One need only think of such Sufi leaders as Nizamuddin *Auliya*, "Saints," or the designation of central Asian dervishes as *ishan*, "they."] In Shah ʿAbdul Latif's work, however, this name seems to be an allusion to the manifold manifestations of the Divine in much the same way that his compatriot Qadi Qadan two hundred years earlier saw God as a banyan tree. With its hundreds of above-ground roots, one single banyan tree looks like a forest.

Like her soul sisters, Marui too realizes that her life reaches back to the beginning of creation, to the primordial covenant when God revealed Himself for an instant as Lord to the newly emerging race of man. They would owe Him obedience from that moment on until the end of time, until judgment day.

Marui suffers exactly as do Sassi and Sohni. Every loving soul knows "there is no love except that for the First Beloved," and the reference to the *alastu* of the primordial covenant not only permeates the first part of this *Sur* but echoes again at its end:

> "Am I not your Lord?"
> Thus I heard the voice of God.
> They said: "Yes!" With all my heart
>   I was the one who said that.
>   From that moment on I pledged
> my love to the forest dwellers.

But that's not all, for already before this wondrous event, even before the sun and the moon were created, before the world came into being and the human spirit created, even before God uttered the divine command "Be!" even then Marui loved the Marus, for she was already inseparably bound to them from the beginning of time. The maiden recalls this period of absolute oneness with the One God, the *deus absconditus*, and now grieves over the fact that destiny, here imbued with the specific meaning of "the emergence of creation" which encompasses a duality in itself, separated her from her beloved. Destiny, as she well knows, is "a strong fortress" holding mankind prisoner.

And yet the soul can always find divine words with which to comfort itself in exile. Didn't God say: "We are closer to man than his jugular vein?" (Sura 50:16). Arabic sayings as well as those of the Prophet pop into Marui's mind: "My body is here, but my heart is with You." And all too true is the Arabic lament: "My eyes weep blood when separated from You!"

But didn't the Prophet also say: "All things return to their origins?" Sunk in such thoughts, the unhappy maiden dreams of returning to her roots, to Malir, and the chapter underscores this theme in its concluding chorus:

> Would that I could go home again,
> to the land of my father's toil,
> that I might return to Malir
> and die in the blooming desert soil.

Many of her verses are reminiscent of the songs so familiar to us from Indo-Pakistani folk literature. These were the songs the frequently unhappy brides sang when they suddenly found themselves in their new home dominated by mother- and sisters-in-law. They express a deep yearning for the love of their own parents and siblings. The young Marui often finds her exile unbearable:

> Neither messenger, nor wanderer, nor camelrider come . . .
> No news, no dream, no camelrider comes . . .

Thus she laments in verse after verse. This is a God-forsaken time, the period of the dark night of the soul, devoid of even the smallest sign of mercy from the Beloved Lord that might serve as consolation. Marui's lament "no messenger, no camelrider comes" permeates the later Sindhi poetry as well and reappears most frequently in the lyrics of Sachal Sarmast. Taking up and expanding ʿAbdul Latif's themes, Sachal Sarmast endowed his girl-souls with a more ecstatic, a bolder and more passionate expression.

Marui waits in vain, for no one ever comes. When she tries to write a letter to her beloved, her tears fall on the pen and blur the ink.

The motif of waiting for a letter and of the vain attempt to

write a few lines to the Beloved Being is an important theme
in mystical literature. Even the earliest mystical poets considered the lover's tears the only real letters, for, reddened
by the blood of their weeping eyes, they etch on their
parched, parchment-like sallow cheeks "letters that even
the illiterate could read," as the Baghdad mystic Shibli
(d. 945) once put it. Even the Bengali folk poet lets his heroine sing:

> I have made of my fingers a pen
> and of my tears some ink;
> my heart provides the parchment—
> and all of this will I send my Beloved!

In classical poetry the letter carrier is usually a dove or a
pigeon (sending messages via carrier pigeons was highly
developed in medieval Islam), and this messenger was frequently equated with the "dove of the sacred place," which
is just another way to describe the doves that nested in
Mecca and which in fact live in absolute proximity to the
actual religious center, the Kaaba, the "House of God." In
Sind, however, it is the crow (*kang*) that the loving girl
repeatedly enjoins to bring her news of her beloved. As
mentioned earlier in connection with Sassi, the loving
woman promises the messenger bird all kinds of rewards,
and if Sassi offers the bird that lives near her beloved her
own eyes and flesh, then the heroine in Sachal Sarmast's
Sur Malkauns offers sweetmeats and golden threads to
adorn his wings should he but bring her news of her
friends. This very understandable yearning on the part of
the loving soul for a token of favor is expressed in the
invention of ever new names for the "darling crow."

The motif of writing, which for the Sufi included the
ancient symbolism attached to each individual letter, turns
up again and again in Shah ʿAbdul Latif's *Risalo*. After all,
isn't the loving soul bound to her beloved in much the same
way the calligrapher artfully combines the two letters *alif*

and *lam*, *a* and *l*, so that they form the word *la*, "none"—so
that they form, in other words, the beginning of the profession of faith, thus pointing to the fact that there is no other
god except God and no other Beloved except the One,
Primordial and Eternal Divine Beloved?

Given all this, the reader may still be surprised to dis-
cover that the theme of letter writing plays such an important role here, for only a very few people in Sind were able
to read and write at the time. Women were especially and
deliberately kept ignorant of the mysteries of writing "so
that we shouldn't be able to write love letters," as one old
Turkish woman from a very good family once told me with a
mischievous smile. But the letters that Marui expects are
words of grace, and should she want to write, her tears will
serve as ink. Likewise the lyrics of Bullhe Shah proclaim:

> I spend my evenings writing letters,
> for my Beloved has not come.

In the absence of news from her village and of dreams
disclosing her beloved, Marui still has her memories of
home to fall back upon. She recalls how the shepherds in
her village never wear silk, and yet how much more beautiful are their coarse red woolen blankets than the precious
shawls, the velvets, and the silks with which Omar tries to
seduce her! And how much more pleasant is their scent
than that of musk and ambergris!

The fact that Marui remembers particularly the scents
and smells of her homeland is not without significance. The
Sufis frequently experienced the soft wafts of scent that
God bestowed upon their souls as harbingers of news of the
invisible beloved—fragrant waves of familiarity and beauty.
Didn't the Prophet sense the sweet-smelling breeze that
brought him news of the pious Uways al-Qarani of Yemen
when he exclaimed: "The breath of the Merciful comes to
me from Yemen?" This may be the idea informing Marui's

yearnings for the "fragrance of friendship" meant to console her in her exile.

The Marus in Malir are poor, but Marui perceives this poverty as beautiful and precious, for the Sufi, like the Prophet, is supposed to say: "My poverty is my pride." Although residing in a palace, she dreams of reunion with her girlfriends, for it is sweeter to suffer thirst with one's family than to sup on sherbet! And how could she sleep with an easy mind under warm comforters knowing her friends are wandering about in the wilderness and sleeping in the cold dew?

She rejects all the gifts Omar offers her, for the soul is not supposed to yield to the temptations of the "beautified joys of the world" (Sura 3:14) and thus forget its true home. Marui prefers to neglect herself completely; she greets the necklaces Omar gives her with indifference, refuses all gifts, and turns her face homeward. The fire of separation burns in her heart; its pain smolders. Her face becomes dirty, for the soul in exile changes its color and loses its glow. Fear overwhelms her when she ponders how she might possibly return to her homeland in her current ugly state, for there everything beams in its primordial beauty. This might be a reference to another of the Sufis' favorite sayings: "Verily, God is beautiful and He loves beauty."

Thus, the almost despairing Marui sits in the prison of the world—and be this prison as richly decorated as Omar's tent!—and sings wistfully:

> I have lost my beauty
>> and am dirty to behold;
>> how can I go to the place
> where never the uncomely come?

> I have lost my beauty,
>> the lovely glow of loveliness;
>> my heart seethes in the vapors of agony
> my countenance has been soiled.

I have lost my beauty—
>   and I've just arrived here!
>   How can I regain what is lost?
Here my beauty vanished without a trace.

I have lost my beauty—
>   where has my perfection flown?
How can I ever go back home
>   when I'm as miserable as I am?
>   Who will give me back my beauty
so that I can face the shepherds?

I have lost my beauty—
>   how can I go back home?
>   I, from whom beauty was taken,
how can I look at the shepherds?

I have lost my beauty—
>   how can I glimpse the shepherds?
>   The one who used to delight the shepherds
now grieves in a deformed state!

I have lost my beauty—
>   who should receive me now?
>   There'll be no joy, no loving embrace
when the shepherds spy this ugly face!

I have lost my beauty—
>   only yesterday did I enter this palace:
>   odious both presents and patronage—
here my beauty has faded away!

Marui stops washing her hair (a very grave sign, given Islam's strict rules about personal hygiene). She now abandons all hope that the friends she loved so long will even recognize her in her present state of unkempt ugliness. She recalls the days she used to churn the curds and whey and fetch water from the fountain to soothe the thirsty cattle — and the following chapters are filled with descriptions of village life and activities: the dress, the plants, the animals of the Thar. In fact, they paint such a realistic picture of life in a desert village far removed from civilization that to this day one can still find there all the herbs and ingredients mentioned in these chapters.

If urbane poets can compare primordial paradise to a rose garden to which the nightingale-soul yearns to return, or to a reed bed from which the lamenting flutes have been cut, one should have no difficulty in appreciating Marui's representation of the "village of her ancestors" as the place of eternal happiness. She remembers how the falling rain turns the steppes into a verdant green and how the Marus rejoice at such times. After all, as the poets never tire of saying, rain is a sign of *rahmat*, divine mercy. In his *Sur Sarang*, Shah ʿAbdul Latif gives a detailed description of the land where everything—"frog, duck, ox and cow," even the peasant—yearns for blessing-bestowing rains and rejoices when they come, for rain is the symbol of divine mercy as embodied in the Prophet Muhammad. It is not necessary for the modern reader to appreciate rain in this metaphorical sense, but whoever has seen the Thar Desert right after the heavy monsoon rains knows how bewitchingly beautiful it is and can surely understand Marui's longing for her homeland. In the end, then, Marui's story is not just another example of the loving soul yearning for its First Beloved, but also a hymn of homesickness, for didn't the Prophet say "love of one's home is part of faith?"

When Marui thinks about this period of grace in her homeland, she weeps like a cloud herself, longing for the arrival of a messenger. She closes herself off from everything, for she wants to remain pure and unsullied by all earthly desires. She finally gets her reward: the Marus send a messenger, and in the rainy season Omar agrees to send her back home. In classical Indian poetry the rainy season is always the period of deepest longing for the beloved, a time that harbors the deepest hopes for union. Happily,

Marui pictures how "everyone will drink milk" upon her return; a huge feast will be celebrated close to the wells the rains have refilled.

The rain theme crops up yet again, this time in an image unusual for a desert landscape but one that is ubiquitous in classical Islamic literature as well as in the folk tradition. The raindrop, so the belief goes, rises from the ocean, the dampness condenses to a cloud and then falls back into the sea in the form of rain. If lucky, the raindrop falls into the oyster that has been waiting longingly for it, for this oyster has refused to drink the salt water surrounding it, preferring to wait for pure sweet rainwater instead, most preferably that of the salubrious April showers. Marui is likened to one of these oysters—she has not yielded to the temptation of the salt water surrounding her, which is to say, she has not succumbed to Omar's glory and the presents he showers upon her. This "comely patience" (Sura 12:18) has led her to her goal and at the same time turned her into a model for all humankind.

> Oysters at the bottom of the sea
>   invest all their hopes in the clouds;
> refusing the briny sea
>   they open themselves only to sweet water
>   thus acquiring the pearl as reward
> for the ordeals they suffered in the darkest depths.
>
> Learn from the oyster, Oh maidens,
>   what virtue is all about;
>   though the tide may ebb and flow,
> they stand fast, waiting for the cloud.
>
>   So learn the ways of yearning,
> Oh maidens, from the oysters
>   that beg sweet water from Heaven
> while disdaining the brine surrounding them.

Marui also knows that her exile was necessary. The trials this pure maiden had to endure are an honor for the true believer, for there is no ascent without pain and suffering. Rumi, like all the other mystical poets, never tired of reminding his listeners that one must be torn from one's roots (i.e., separated from one's native land) before one can grow and develop. After all, didn't the Prophet leave his native Mecca to become ruler in Medina and only after that return in triumph to his homeland? And isn't the same true of Yusuf, who, because of his brothers' treachery, eventually became the "Mighty One of Egypt," able to comfort and console his people who hailed from the same homeland? Could the reed-pipe sing if it hadn't been cut off from its roots?

Marui's perseverance, her loyalty, is rewarded in this same way: unsullied by the world, unspoiled by the glorious seductions of exile, she returns to the village of her ancestors, to the womb of her primordial homeland.

⟶ Epilogue ⟶

MARUI YEARNS FOR HER PRIMORDIAL HOMELAND, and Sassi and Sohni are as purified by their yearning for the Divine Beloved as is Zulaikha by her passion for Yusuf. Just as they all yearn for their origin, the All-Encompassing Beauty, so women in the mystical tradition in general can be looked upon as the most attractive, pleasantly fragrant manifestations of the One. Not only does the part (which is to say, the woman, first created from Adam's rib) seek the whole, but the whole is also searching for that part which has been separated from it. Man and woman are inextricably bound to each other, and only their harmonious co-existence, the eternally creative play between *yang* and *yin*, is what makes up life as we know it.

The fact that the male principle repeatedly dominates, at least in the practical aspects of living, is a given in all religions and cultures, and it is undeniable that in Islam, too, much suffering has fallen to the lot of women because simple Quranic precepts have been interpreted more and more narrowly over the course of time. Moreover, customs and attitudes lacking any and all Quranic foundation have become increasingly rigid. This rigidity, in turn, has taken on an almost canonical character. Much of what is represented as "Islamic" today stems from these increasingly petrifying stratifications. On the other hand, we have to be careful not to look upon our ideas that stem from a liberal, frequently from an "uninhibited" interpretation of the concept "freedom," as ideals applicable and valid for all the world. We have to be equally wary not to dismiss or condemn outright as being old-fashioned customs and habits we happen not to like. Muslims easily reject the transposition of certain "modern" ideals onto the Islamic world as being just another new attempt at colonization. Such perceptions do little more than engender sharp resistance.

Historians of religion should continue to observe the rule that requires ideal be compared with ideal, reality with reality. That's why I believe a careful study of the image of women in Islamic literature can help us better appreciate these ideals. Neither lascivious harem eroticism nor popular anecdotes about the cunning of womankind have determined the culture of Islam. Those who read the classical works of the Arabic, Persian, Turkish, and especially the Indo-Muslim world with an open eye and an open mind—and this includes works in Urdu, Sindhi, Panjabi, and other languages—will arrive at a completely different image from the one they are likely to find "on the street," as it were. And during the many years in which I have shared the friendship of Muslim women, I have learned a great deal about these deeper levels. Perhaps one such insight can help set some of the prejudices aright, at least to a certain extent; after all, there ought to exist no difference between man and woman in the realm of spiritual life. As Jami says of the great Rabiʿa,

> If all women were like the one we have mentioned,
> then women would be preferred to men.
> For the feminine gender is no shame for the sun,
> nor is the masculine gender an honor for the moon.[1]

---

[1] Quoted in Annemarie Schimmel, *Mystical Dimensions of Islam* (Chapel Hill, N.C., 1975), p. 435.

Bibliography

ʿAbdul Latif, Shah. *Risalo Sindhi.* Edited by Kalyan Adwani. Bombay, 1958.

Abu Nuʿaim al-Isfahani. *Hilyat al-auliya*, 10 vols. Cairo, 1932–.

Addas, Claude. *Ibn Arabi, ou, La quête du Soufre Rouge: Quest for the Red Sulphur: The Life of Ibn Arabi.* Translated from the French into English by Peter Kingsley. Cambridge, 1993.

Aflaki. *Manaqib al-ʿarifin.* Edited by Tahsin Yazici. 2 vols. Ankara, 1959–61.

Allison, Mary Bruins, M.D. *Doctor Mary in Arabia: Memoirs.* Austin, n.d.

Andrae, Tor. *I myrtenträdgården.* Translated from the Swedish into English by Birgitta Sharpe with foreword by Annemarie Schimmel: *In the Garden of Myrtles: Studies in Early Islamic Mysticism.* Albany, 1987.

Amir Khurd. *Siyar al-auliya.* Delhi, 1310h/1891–92.

ʿAndalib, Nasir Muhammad. *Nala-i ʿAndalib.* Bhopal, 1309h/1890–91.

Araz, Nezihe. *Anadolu Evliyalari.* Istanbul, 1958.

Arberry, A. J. *A Sufi Martyr: The* Apologia *of ʿAin al-Qudat al-Hamadhani.* London, 1969.

Asani, Ali S. "Bridal Symbolism in the Ismaili *ginan* Literature." In *Mystics of the Book*, by R. Herrera and Ruth Link Salinger. New York, 1993.

———. *The Buj Niranjan, an Ismaili mystical Poem.* Harvard Middle East Center, Cambridge, Mass., 1991.

————. "The Ismaili *ginans* as Devotional Literature." In *Devotional Literature in South Asia*, edited by S. McGregor. Cambridge, 1993.

————. "A Testimony of Love: The Git Tradition of the Nizari Ismailis." In *Festschrift für Annemarie Schimmel*, edited by Maria Subtelny, *Journal of Turkish Studies* 18. Cambridge, Mass., 1994.

Asi, ʿAbdul Bari. *Tadhkirat al-Khawatin*. Lucknow, ca. 1930.

ʿAttar, Farid al-Din. *The Ilahi-nama or Book of God of Farid al-Din ʿAttar*. Translated from the Persian by John Andrew Boyle, with foreword by Annemarie Schimmel. Manchester, 1976.

————. *Mantiq al-tayr*. English translation with an introduction by Afkham Darbandi and Dick Davis: *The Conference of the Birds*. New York, 1984.

————. *Musibatnama*. Edited by N. Wisal. Tehran, 1959. Partial French translation by Isabelle de Gastines: *Le Livre de l'épreuve*. Paris, 1981.

————. *Tadhkirat al-auliya*. Edited by R. A. Nicholson. 2 vols. London/Leiden, 1905, 1907. Reprint, 1959.

Austin, R. W. J. "The Sophianic Feminine in the Work of Ibn al-ʿArabi and Rumi." In *The Legacy of Mediaeval Persian Sufism*, edited by L. Lewisohn. London, 1991.

————. *Sufis of Andalusia*. London, 1971.

Ayoub, Mahmood. *Redemptive Suffering in Islam*. The Hague, 1978.

Ayverdi, Samiha: *Ibrahim Efendi'nin Konagi*. Istanbul, 1964.

————. *Istanbul Geceleri*. Istanbul, 1952.

Badawi, M. M. "Islam in Modern Egyptian Literature." *Journal of Arabic Literature* 2 (1971).

Baha-i Walad. *Maʿarif*. Edited by B. Furuzanfar. Teheran, 1957.

Bannerth, Ernst. *Islamische Wallfahrtsstätten Kairos*. Cairo, 1973.

Beaurecueil, Serge de Laurier de. *Abdullah Ansari, mystique hanbalite*. Beirut, 1963.

Beelaert, Anna Livia. "The Kaaba as a Woman—A Topos in Classical Persian Literature." *Persica* 13 (1988/89).

Bilgrami, Ghulam ʿAli Azad. *Khizana-i ʿamira*. Lucknow, ca. 1890.

Birge, John K. *The Bektashi Order of Dervishes*. London, 1937. Reprint, 1965.

Bremond, Henri. *Histoire du sentiment religieux en France*. Volume VI. Paris, 1926.

Bullhe Shah. *Divan*. Edited by Faqir M. Faqir. Lahore, 1960.

Burton, Richard. *Sindh, and the Races that Inhabit the Valley of the Indus*. London, 1851. Reprint, 1974.

Chittick, William. *The Sufi Path of Knowledge*. Albany, 1989.

Chodkiewicz, Michel. "Female Sainthood in Islam." *SUFI* 21 (1994). This is an excellent introduction to the topic.

———. *An Ocean without Shore: Ibn Arabi, The Book, and The Law*. Albany, 1993.

Cooke, Miriam, and Roshni Rustomji-Kerns, eds. *Blood into Ink: South Asian and Middle Eastern Women Write War*. Boulder, 1994.

Dailami, Abu'l Hasan ad-. *Sirat Ibn al-Khafif-i Shirazi*. Edited by A. Schimmel. Ankara, 1955.

Dara Shikoh. *Sakinat al-auliya*. Edited by Jalali Naini. Teheran, 1965.

Dard, Khwadja Mir. *Divan-i Farsi*. Delhi, 1891.

———. *'Ilm ul-kitab*. Bhopal, 1309h/1890–91.

Diederichs, Inge, ed. *Im Lande der Königin von Saba*. Cologne, 1987.

Eaton, Richard. *Sufis of Bijapur*. Princeton, 1978.

Enamul Haq. *Muslim Bengali Literature*. Karachi, 1957.

Ethé, Hermann. "Neupersische Literatur." In *Grundriß der iranischen Philologie*, vol. 2, by Wilhelm Geiger-Ernst Kuhn. Strasbourg, 1901.

Fakhri Haravi. *Javahir al-ajayib* (together with Raudat as-salatin). Edited by Sayyid Hussam al-Din Rashidi. Hyderabad/Sind, 1968.

Fazlur Rahman. *Islam*. London/New York, 1966.

Ghazzali, Abu Hamid al-. *Ihya' 'ulum ad-din*. 4 volumes. Bulaq, 1872.

Ghazzali, Ahmad ibn Muhammad. *Sawanih*. English translation from the Persian with a commentary and notes by Nasrollah Pourjavady: *Sawanih: Inspirations from the World of Pure Spirits: The Oldest Persian Sufi Treatise on Love*. New York, 1986.

Ghulam Farid, Khwaja. *Fifty Poems.* Edited and translated by Christopher Shackle. Multan, ca. 1975.

Gibb, E. J. W. *History of Ottoman Poetry.* 6 volumes. London/Leiden, 1900–1909. Reprint, 1958–63.

Gölpinarli, Abdulbaki. *Mevlâna'dan sonra Mevlevilik.* Istanbul, 1953

———. *Tasavvuftan dilimize geçen terimler.* Istanbul, 1977.

Gost, Roswitha. *Der Harem.* Cologne, 1994.

Gramlich, Richard. *Die Gaben der Erkenntnisse des 'Umar as Suhrawardi.* Wiesbaden, 1978. Translation of Suhrawardi's *'awarif al-ma'arif.*

———. *Die schiitischen Derwischorden.* 3 vols. Wiesbaden, 1965–81.

———. *Die Wunder der Freunde Gottes.* Stuttgart, 1987.

Hallaj, al-Husain ibn Mansur. *Diwan.* Edited by Louis Massignon. *Journal Asiatique* (1931), edited by M. Kamil ash- Shaibi. Beirut, 1973.

Hammer, Joseph von. *Der Diwan des . . . Hafis: Aus dem Persischen . . .* Stuttgart, 1812–13.

Heine, Ina, and Peter Heine. *O ihr Musliminnen! Frauen in islamischen Gesellschaften.* Freiburg, 1994.

Heller, Erdmute, and Hassouna Mosbahi. *Hinter den Schleiern des Islam.* Munich, 1993.

Hoshyarpuri, Hafeez. *Mathnawiha-yi Hir Ranjha.* Karachi, 1957.

Hujwiri, Ali ibn 'Usman. *The Kashf al-mahjub: The Oldest Persian Treatise on Sufiism, Written by Ali ibn Uthman al-Hujwiri.* Translated by Reynold A. Nicholson. London/Leiden, 1911.

Ibn al-'Arabi. *Fusus al-hikam.* Edited by A. A. Affifi. Cairo, 1946.

———. *Turjuman al-ashwaq: A Collection of Mystical Odes.* Edited and translated by R. A. Nicholson. London, 1912. Reprinted with foreword by Martin Lings. London, 1978.

Ibn 'Ata 'Allah. *Hikam: Bedrängnisse sind Teppiche voller Gnaden.* Translated into German by Annemarie Schimmel. Freiburg, 1988.

Ibn Iyas. *Bada'i' az-zuhur fi waqa'i' ad-duhur,* Volumes 3–5. Edited by M. Mostafa and Paul Kahle. Istanbul/Leipzig, 1931–35.

Ibn Khallikan. *Wafayat al-a'yan.* Edited by M. G. de Slane. Paris,
    1838–42.
Iqbal, Muhammad. *Bang-i dara.* Lahore, 1924.
———. *Javidnama.* Lahore, 1932. German translation by
    Annemarie Schimmel: *Buch der Ewigkeit.* Munich, 1957. Also
    in *Botschaft des Ostens.* Tübingen, 1977.
———. *Payam-i mashriq.* Lahore, 1923.
———. *Rumuz-i bekhudi.* Lahore, 1917.
Jami, Maulana 'Abdur Rahman. *Masnavi-i haft awrang.* Edited by
    Aga Murtaza and Mudarris-i Gilani. Teheran, 1972. Includes:
    Salaman wa Absal; Silsilat al-dhahab; Subhat al-abrar; Yusuf
    wa Zulaykha.
———. *Nafahat al-uns.* Edited by M. Tauhidipur. Teheran, 1957.
Jotwani, Motilal. *Shah Abdul Karim: A Mystic Poet of Sindh.* New
    Delhi, 1970.
Kadin Sairleri Altari. In *Sombahar,* nos. 21–22 (January–April
    1994). Istanbul.
Karaosmanoğlu, Yakup Kadri. *Nur Baba.* Istanbul, 1922. German
    translation by Annemarie Schimmel: *Flamme und Falter.*
    Cologne, 1987.
Khaqani, Afdaluddin Badil. *Divan.* Edited by Z. Sajjadi. Teheran,
    1959.
Kisai, Muhammad ibn Abd Allah al-. *The Tales of the Prophets.*
    Translated into English by Wheeler M. Thackston, Jr. Boston,
    1978.
Lawrence, Bruce B. "Honoring Women through Sexual Absti-
    nence." In *Festschrift für Annemarie Schimmel,* edited by
    Maria Subtelny, *Journal of Turkish Studies* 18. Cambridge,
    Mass., 1994.
Massignon, Louis. *Passion de Husayn Ibn Mansur Hallaj.* Trans-
    lated into English and edited by Herbert Mason: *The Passion
    of Al-Hallaj: Mystic and Martyr of Islam.* Princeton, 1994.
Meier, Fritz. *Abu Sa'id-i Abu l-Hair.* Leiden, 1976.
———. *Baha-i Walad.* Leiden, 1990.
———. *Die schöne Mahsati.* Wiesbaden, 1963.
Mernissi, Fatima. *Dreams of Trespass: Tales of a Harem Girlhood.*
    Reading, 1994.
Metcalf, Barbara. *Perfecting Women: Maulana Ashraf Ali Tha-
    nawi's Bihishti Zewar.* Delhi, 1992.

Mez, Adam. *The Renaissance of Islam.* English translation by
    Salahuddin Khuda Bukhsh and D. S. Margoliouth. Beirut,
    1973.

Murata, Sachiko. "Mysteries of Marriage: Notes on a Sufi Text
    (Kasani)." In *The Legacy of Mediaeval Persian Sufism,* edited
    by L. Lewisohn. London, 1992.

———. *The Tao of Islam.* Albany, 1992.

———. "Witnessing the Rose: Yaqub Sarfi on the Vision of God in
    Women." In Alma Giese and J. C. Bürgel, "Gott ist schön und
    Er liebt die Schönheit" in *Festschrift für Annemarie Schimmel.*
    Bern/Frankfurt, 1994.

Nahj al-balagha, with commentary by Muhammad ʿAbduh. Beirut,
    1964.

Nazir Ahmad, Dept. *Mirʾat al-ʿarus.* Delhi, 1869.

Nizami, Ilyas. "Makhzan al-asrar." In *Khamsa,* 3rd ed. Teheran,
    1972.

Nizami, Khaliq Ahmad. *The Life and Times of Shaikh Farid Ganj-i
    Shakar.* Aligarh, 1955.

Nizamuddin Auliya. *Fawaʾid al-fuʾad.* Translated into English and
    annotated by Bruce B. Lawrence, with an introduction by
    Khaliq Ahmad Nizami: *Nizam ad-din Awliya: Morals for the
    Heart: Conversations of Shaykh Nizam ad-din Awliya
    recorded by Amir Hasan Sijzi.* New York, 1992.

Prior, Loveday. *Punjab Prelude.* London, 1952.

Qalich Beg, Mirza. *Zinat.* Karachi, 1892.

Qalqashandi, Ahmad al-. *Subh al-aʿsha.* 14 vols. Cairo, 1915–20.

Quddusi, I. H. *Tadhkira-i sufiya-yi Sind.* Karachi, 1959.

Qushayri, Abd al-Karim ibn Hawazin. *Risalah al-Qushayriyah.*
    Cairo, 1874. German translation by Richard Gramlich: *Das
    Sendschreiben al-Qusvayris über das Sufitum.* Wiesbaden,
    1989.

Ramakrishna, Lajwanti. *Panjabi Sufi Poets.* London/ Calcutta,
    1938. Delhi, 1974. Cf. the article by J. Fück, "Die sufische
    Dichtung in der Landessprache des Panjab." *Orientalische
    Literaturzeitung* 53 (1940).

Reintjes, Hortense. "Der schöne Joseph." In *Festschrift für
    Annemarie Schimmel,* edited by Subtelny. Cambridge, Mass.,
    1994.

Ritter, Hellmut. *Das Meer der Seele: Gott, Welt und Mensch in den Geschichten Fariduddin 'Attars*. Leiden, 1955, 1978.

Rumi, Jalal al-Din: *Divan-i kabir ya kulliyat-i Shams*. Edited by B. Furuzanfar. 10 vols. Teheran, 1957–75.

———. *Fihi ma fihi*. Edited by B. Furuzanfar. Teheran, 1959. German translation by Annemarie Schimmel: *Von Allem und vom Einen*. Munich, 1987.

———. *Mathnawi-yi maʿnawi*. Edited, translated into English and annotated by R. A. Nicholson. 8 vols. Leiden/London, 1925–40. Partial German translation by Annemarie Schimmel: *Das Mathnawi*. Basel, 1994.

Sachal Sarmast. *Risalo Sindhi*. Edited by O. A. Ansari. Karachi, 1958.

———. *Siraiki kalam*. Edited by Maulwi H. A. Sadiq Ranipuri. Karachi, 1959.

Sanaʾi, Abu l-Majd Majdud. *Divan*. Edited by M. Razawi. Teheran, 1950.

———. *Hadiqat al-haqiqa*. Edited by M. Razawi. Teheran, 1961.

Sauda, Mirza ʿAbdul Qadir. *Kulliyat*. Edited by Khurshidul Islam. Aligarh, 1965.

Shariati, Ali. *Fatimah Fatimah ast*. English translation by Laleh Bakhtiar: *Ali Shariati's Fatima Is Fatima*. Teheran, 1981.

Schimmel, Annemarie. *Al-Halladsch, Märtyrer der Gottesliebe*. Cologne, 1969.

———. *And Muhammad Is His Messenger: The Veneration of the Prophet in Islamic Piety*. Chapel Hill, 1985.

———. *As through a Veil: Mystical Poetry in Islam*. New York, 1982.

———. *Aus dem Goldenen Becher: Türkische Lyrik vom 13. bis zum 20. Jahrhundert*. 3rd expanded ed. Cologne, 1992.

———. "Classical Urdu Literature." In *History of Indian Literature*, edited by J. Gonda. Wiesbaden, 1974–75.

———. "Ein Frauenbildungsroman auf Sindhi: Mirza Qalich Begs Zinat." *Der Islam* 39 (1964).

———. "Eros—Heavenly and Not-so-Heavenly." In *Society and the Sexes in Medieval Islam*, edited by Afaf L. S. Marsot. Malibu, 1979.

———. "Hochzeitslieder der Frauen im Industal." *Zeitschrift für Volkskunde* 61, 2 (1965).

———. *Islam in the Indian Subcontinent*. Leiden, 1980.

———. *Mystical Dimensions of Islam.* Chapel Hill, 1975.

———. "A Nineteenth-century Anthology of Urdu Poetesses." In *Islamic Society and Culture: Essays in Honour of Aziz Ahmad.* Delhi, 1983.

———. *Pain and Grace: A Study of Two Indo-Muslim Mystical Poets of 18th Century India.* Leiden, 1976.

———. "Samiha Ayverdi, eine Istanbuler Schriftstellerin." In *Festschrift für Otto Spies,* edited by W. Hoernerbach. Wiesbaden, 1967.

———. "Sindhi Literature." In *History of Indian Literature,* edited by J. Gonda. Wiesbaden, 1974–75.

———. *The Triumphal Sun: A Study of the Life and Work of Mowlana Jalaloddin Rumi.* 2nd ed. Albany, 1993.

———. *Unendliche Suche: Geschichten des Schah Abdul Latif von Sind.* Munich, 1983.

———. *Von Ali bis Zahra: Namen und Namengebung im Islam.* Munich, 1993.

———. "Women in Mystical Islam." *Women's Studies International Forum* 5/11 (1982).

———. *Zeitgenössische arabische Lyrik* in German translation. Tübingen, 1975.

Smith, Margaret. *Rabia the Mystic and Her Fellow Saints in Islam.* Cambridge, 1928–.

Sorley, Herbert T. *Shah Abdul Latif of Bhit.* Oxford, 1940. Reprint, 1966.

Sprenger, Aloys. *A Catalogue of the Arabic, Persian and Hindustany Manuscripts in the Libraries of the Kings of Oudh.* Calcutta, 1854. Reprint, 1979.

Stowasser, Barbara Freyer. *Women in the Qurʾan, Traditions and Interpretations.* New York, 1994.

Suhrawardi, Shihabaddin. *The Mystical and Visionary Treatises of Shihabuddin Yahya Suhrawardi.* Translated by Wheeler M. Thackston, Jr. London, 1982.

———. *Oeuvres en Persan.* Edited by Henry Corbin. Paris, 1970.

Sulami. *Tabaqat as-sufiya.* Edited by N. Shariba. Cairo, 1953.

Ter Haar, Jon. "The Importance of the Spiritual Guide in the Naqshbandi Order." In *The Legacy of Mediaeval Persian Sufism,* edited by L. Lewisohn. London, 1992.

Thanawi, Ashraf ʿAli. *Bihishti Zewar.* Cf. Metcalf.

Tirmidhi, al-Hakim al-. *Khatam al-auliya.* Edited by Osman Yahya. Beirut, 1965.

Troll, Christian W. *Muslim Shrines in India.* Delhi, 1989.

Vaudeville, Charlotte. *Barahmasa in Indian Literatures: Songs of the Twelve Months in Indo-Aryan Literatures.* Delhi, 1986.

Vaughan-Lee, Llewellyn. "The People of the Secret." *Sufi* 22 (Summer 1994).

Walther, Wiebke. *Die Frau im Islam.* English translation by C. S. V. Salt: *Woman in Islam.* Montclair, 1981.

Waris Shah. *The Adventures of Hir & Ranjha. [A Translation into English Prose by Ch. Frederick Usborne, from the Panjabi Poem of Waris Shah].* Edited with an introduction and notes by Mumtaz Hasan. Karachi, 1966.

Yashrutiyya, Fatima al-. *Rihla ila'l-haqq.* Beirut, ca. 1955.

Young, William C. "The Ka'ba, Gender, and the Rites of Pilgrimage." *International Journal of Middle East Studies* 25 (1993).

Zaidi, M. H. *Katalog der Urdu-Handschriften in deutschen Bibliotheken. Nr. 64: fawa'id an nisa.* Wiesbaden, 1973.

▲ Index of Names ▲